They're Lying to You: Understanding Propaganda Techniques

by
Victor Langley

Victor Langley

This book is dedicated to those
who seek the truth. May you always find it.

Table of Contents

INTRO

The Power and Peril of Persuasion

In an era where information flows freely and ceaselessly, a single tweet can spark a global movement, and a well-crafted narrative can shape the course of history. Welcome to the age of persuasion, where the line between truth and manipulation often blurs, leaving us vulnerable to the machinations of those who seek to sway our thoughts and actions.

There was a recent foreign election where a viral video purportedly showing a candidate accepting bribes turned the tide of public opinion overnight. The video, later proven to be a sophisticated deepfake, had already done its damage. Millions of voters, influenced by this fabricated evidence, cast their ballots based on a lie.

This incident is just one example of the pervasive nature of propaganda in our modern world. From social media echo chambers to carefully orchestrated news cycles, we are constantly bombarded with information designed to influence our beliefs and behaviors. The techniques used are varied and often subtle: emotional appeals that bypass our rational thinking, social proof that exploits our need for conformity, and misinformation that capitalizes on our cognitive biases.

As we navigate this complex landscape, the ability to recognize and analyze propaganda becomes not just an academic exercise, but a vital skill for informed citizenship. This book serves as your guide, a toolkit to help you discern fact from fiction, truth from distortion. By understanding the machinery of influence, you'll be better equipped to make decisions based on reality rather than manipulation.

In the chapters that follow, we'll explore the myriad forms of propaganda, from ancient techniques to cutting-edge digital strategies. You'll learn to spot the telltale signs of manipulation and develop the critical thinking skills necessary to question the narratives presented to you. Our journey together will empower you to become not just a consumer of information, but a discerning analyst of the world around you.

The stakes have never been higher. In an age where democracy itself can be swayed by the power of persuasion, your ability to think critically is your greatest defense. Let's embark on this exploration together, and unmask the machinery of influence that shapes our world.

They're Lying to You

Chapter 1: Defining and Historical Context of Propaganda

In the complex world of human communication, one thread stands out for its profound impact on society: propaganda. This term, often shrouded in negative connotations, encompasses a range of messages and strategies designed to influence public perception, shape opinions, and incite action. Propaganda is not confined to a singular domain; rather, it manifests in various forms across political, commercial, and social landscapes. From fervent political speeches that rally a nation behind a cause to cleverly crafted advertisements that entice consumers to purchase the latest product, propaganda is an omnipresent force that permeates many aspects of life.

To fully appreciate the significance of propaganda, one must recognize its pervasive nature in contemporary society. Whether through traditional media channels such as television and print or through the ever-evolving digital platforms, the mechanisms of propaganda are employed with increasing sophistication. In an age where information travels faster than ever before, the potential for propaganda to shape public discourse has intensified. Social media platforms, for instance, have become hotbeds for propaganda, enabling individuals, organizations, and even governments to disseminate messages that can rapidly gain traction and influence vast audiences. The lines between information, misinformation, and propaganda can often blur, leading to a challenging landscape for discerning truth from manipulation.

As we look deeper into the concept of propaganda, it is essential to establish a comprehensive definition. At its core, propaganda is a form of communication aimed at persuading an audience to adopt a particular viewpoint or take a specific action. It often employs various techniques, including emotional appeals, selective presentation of facts, and repetition, to reinforce its message. While propaganda can be used for noble causes, such as promoting public health initiatives or encouraging civic engagement, it can also be wielded as a tool of manipulation, fostering division and reinforcing harmful stereotypes.

The etymology of the term "propaganda" provides further insight into its multifaceted nature. The word itself is derived from the Latin term "propagare," meaning to propagate, spread, or disseminate. The modern usage of the term traces back to the 17th century, with the establishment of the Congregatio de Propaganda Fide, a congregation of the Catholic Church responsible for spreading the faith and countering the Protestant Reformation. This early iteration of propaganda was deeply intertwined with religious and political objectives, aiming to influence the beliefs and behaviors of individuals and communities in favor of Catholicism.

As we navigate the historical landscape of propaganda, it becomes evident that its evolution has mirrored the changing dynamics of society and communication. The early 20th century marked a significant turning point, particularly during periods of conflict. Wartime propaganda played a crucial role in shaping public sentiment and mobilizing nations for the war effort. Governments recognized the power of propaganda as a means to foster unity, galvanize support for military campaigns, and demonize the enemy. In this context, propaganda took on a more organized and systematic approach, with governments employing specialized agencies to craft and disseminate messages that would resonate with the populace.

The impact of wartime propaganda can be observed through various case studies. For instance, during World War I, the United States established the Committee on Public Information (CPI), tasked with generating support for the war through a series of persuasive campaigns. The CPI leveraged a diverse array of media, including pamphlets, posters, films, and speeches, to galvanize public opinion in favor of the war effort. Iconic images, such as the "I Want You" recruitment poster featuring Uncle Sam, became emblematic of this propaganda campaign, effectively appealing to the patriotic sentiments of American citizens.

The transition to the digital age has brought forth a new era of propaganda, fundamentally altering the way messages are constructed and disseminated. The rise of social media platforms has democratized communication, enabling individuals and organizations to bypass traditional media gatekeepers and reach global audiences with unprecedented speed. This shift has not only expanded the reach of propaganda but has also intensified the competition for attention in an increasingly crowded information landscape. The algorithms that govern social media platforms often prioritize sensational and emotionally charged content, inadvertently amplifying propaganda that exploits these dynamics.

Case studies from recent years illustrate the transformative effects of digital propaganda on public opinion. The 2016 United States presidential election serves as a poignant example, whereby social media platforms became battlegrounds for competing narratives. The use of targeted advertisements, misinformation campaigns, and the strategic manipulation of algorithms played pivotal roles in shaping voter perceptions and influencing electoral outcomes. As algorithms curate news feeds based on user preferences, individuals may find themselves in echo chambers, where their beliefs are reinforced rather than challenged. This phenomenon raises critical questions about the role of propaganda in a digital age characterized by information overload and polarized discourse.

As we explore the historical evolution of propaganda, it is essential to acknowledge its dual nature. On one hand, propaganda can serve as a catalyst for positive change, promoting awareness of social issues and mobilizing communities for collective action. On the other hand, it can be weaponized to distort reality, sow discord, and manipulate public sentiment for ulterior motives. The challenge lies in navigating this complex terrain, discerning between constructive messaging and harmful manipulation.

The historical context of propaganda is rich and varied, providing valuable insights into its enduring influence on society. From its origins in religious endeavors to its contemporary manifestations in political and commercial realms, propaganda has adapted to the changing tides of communication and societal values. As we continue to grapple with the implications of propaganda in our daily lives, it is imperative to cultivate a critical awareness of the messages that permeate our environments. By understanding the historical underpinnings and evolving nature of propaganda, we can better equip ourselves to navigate the challenging landscape of information and discern the motivations behind the messages we encounter.

In concluding this exploration of propaganda's definition and historical context, we stand at a crossroads. The lessons gleaned from the past compel us to recognize the power wielded by those who craft and disseminate messages, urging us to approach information with a discerning eye. The journey through history serves as a reminder that propaganda, while often cloaked in persuasive language, can take on many forms and serve various purposes, shaping the narratives that define our shared experiences. As we move forward, it is incumbent upon each of us to remain vigilant, questioning the motives behind the messages that permeate our lives and striving to foster a society where truth prevails over manipulation.

As we transition into a deeper examination of propaganda's evolution through different eras, we will uncover the nuances that characterize its development and the pivotal moments that have shaped its trajectory. By analyzing historical contexts, case studies, and the profound impact of propaganda on public opinion, we will gain a clearer understanding of its role in shaping our world today. The journey through history beckons, inviting us to explore the intricate dance between communication, persuasion, and the ever-evolving landscape of human thought.

In our exploration of propaganda, we have journeyed through its historical roots, various forms, and its pervasive presence across cultures and political landscapes. However, to fully grasp its significance and impact on society, it is essential to look deeper into the psychological mechanisms that underlie propaganda's effectiveness, as well as the social dynamics and ethical implications that arise from its use. This chapter aims to dissect these dimensions, ensuring that we are equipped with a comprehensive understanding of how propaganda operates on both a psychological and ethical plane, and how it influences our perceptions, beliefs, and behaviors in profound ways.

To begin with, we must acknowledge that propaganda is not merely a collection of messages designed to sway public opinion; it is a sophisticated interplay of psychological tactics that leverages our inherent cognitive biases and emotional responses. Understanding these psychological dynamics allows us to see how propaganda not only shapes opinions but also molds our very identities and interpersonal relationships within society.

At the heart of propaganda lies the use of emotional appeals, which often serve as powerful catalysts for persuasion. Propagandists leverage emotions such as fear, anger, and hope to elicit responses that align with their objectives. Fear tactics, in particular, have been instrumental in mobilizing public action and shaping perceptions of threats. For instance, during World War II, governments used fear-based propaganda to galvanize support for military efforts and justify acts of war. Posters depicting the enemy as monstrous or subhuman, along with slogans that emphasized the dangers of complacency, tapped into the collective anxieties of the populace, compelling them to rally behind their nation's cause.

The emotional resonance of such propaganda cannot be overstated. When individuals are confronted with messages that provoke fear, their rational faculties often take a backseat to instinctual responses. This phenomenon is rooted in the brain's limbic system, which governs emotional reactions. The limbic brain acts swiftly, often bypassing the logical, analytical parts of our cognitive processes. Consequently, fear-laden propaganda can effectively short-circuit critical thinking, leading individuals to accept assertions without rigorous scrutiny, thereby fostering a fertile ground for misinformation and manipulation.

Moreover, the influence of authority figures serves as another critical psychological lever within the propaganda landscape. The principle of authority suggests that individuals are more likely to accept information and directives from those deemed credible or powerful. This dynamic can be observed in various contexts, from political leaders to celebrities endorsing products or ideologies. The mere presence of an authority figure can imbue a message with legitimacy, creating a halo effect that obscures potential flaws in reasoning.

A poignant historical example is the use of propaganda by figures such as Joseph Goebbels, the Nazi Minister of Propaganda, during World War II. Goebbels understood the psychology of authority and utilized it masterfully to instill loyalty to the regime. He curated a narrative that positioned Adolf Hitler as a larger-than-life figure, effectively framing him as an infallible leader whose decisions were to be followed without question. This manipulation of authority not only silenced dissent but also fostered an environment in which individuals willingly accepted increasingly draconian measures in the name of national security and unity.

As we navigate the complex terrain of propaganda, it is crucial to recognize the cognitive biases that further facilitate its acceptance. Confirmation bias, for instance, refers to the tendency to seek out or interpret information in a manner that confirms our pre-existing beliefs. This bias creates a scenario in which individuals gravitate toward propaganda that resonates with their worldview, effectively filtering out contradictory information. In an age where information is abundant and often conflicting, confirmation bias serves as a powerful ally for propagandists, allowing them to craft narratives that reinforce existing beliefs and further entrench individuals within ideological silos.

Another relevant cognitive bias is the bandwagon effect, which underscores our propensity to adopt beliefs or behaviors simply because we perceive others doing so. The bandwagon effect is particularly pronounced in group settings, where individuals may conform to the prevailing opinions or actions of their peers, often without critical evaluation. This phenomenon can be manipulated through propaganda by creating the illusion of widespread support for a particular idea or policy, thereby pressuring others to join the chorus. The bandwagon effect can thus create echo chambers that perpetuate misinformation, leading to a reinforcing cycle of belief that distorts reality.

Together, these psychological dynamics create a complex web that underpins the effectiveness of propaganda. During World War II, the use of emotional appeals, authority figures, and cognitive biases all played a crucial role in shaping public opinion and mobilizing nations. The emotional weight of propaganda posters, coupled with the authoritative voices of military leaders, created a narrative that many could not resist. As we examine this historical context, it becomes clear that the psychological dimensions of propaganda are not merely theoretical constructs; they have real-world implications for how societies respond to crises, governance, and conflict.

However, the exploration of propaganda does not stop at the individual level; it extends into social dynamics that influence how propaganda is disseminated and accepted within groups. The concept of group identity is particularly important, as it shapes the way individuals perceive information and relate to one another within a community. In many cases, propaganda is designed to appeal to group identities, fostering a sense of belonging and solidarity among members of a particular faction or ideology.

Social proof, another salient factor, refers to the phenomenon whereby individuals look to others in their social circles to inform their own opinions and behaviors. This tendency can be exploited by propaganda to create a sense of consensus, even if that consensus is artificially constructed. Social media platforms, in particular, have dramatically amplified these dynamics, as individuals can easily share and disseminate propaganda, often within their own echo chambers. The result is a landscape where misinformation can spread rapidly, unchallenged by dissenting voices, and where individuals may become increasingly insulated from alternative viewpoints.

The rise of social media has ushered in new challenges in this regard. Traditional propaganda techniques have found fertile ground in the digital domain, where algorithms curate content that aligns with user preferences, further entrenching individuals in their beliefs. This can lead to a phenomenon known as "confirmation cascades," where false or misleading information gains traction through repetition within a closed network. As people share content that resonates with their beliefs, they inadvertently create self-reinforcing cycles of misinformation that become increasingly difficult to disrupt.

As we reflect on the social dynamics at play, it is vital to consider the ethical implications surrounding propaganda. Distinguishing between ethical persuasion and manipulation is key to navigating this complex landscape. Ethical persuasion seeks to inform and engage, relying on rational arguments and evidence-based reasoning. In contrast, manipulation exploits emotional vulnerabilities, cognitive biases, and social dynamics to achieve its aims, often at the expense of informed consent and individual autonomy.

The responsibilities of communicators and consumers in an information-saturated environment cannot be overstated. Those who craft messages have an ethical obligation to ensure that their communications are transparent, accurate, and respectful of their audience's capacity for critical thought. Conversely, consumers of information must cultivate a discerning mindset, actively questioning the sources, motivations, and intentions behind the messages they encounter. This critical reflection is essential for preventing the normalization of propaganda and safeguarding the integrity of public discourse.

In an era characterized by rapid technological advancements and an ever-expanding information landscape, the consequences of unchecked propaganda are profound. The proliferation of misinformation can erode trust in institutions, polarize societies, and ultimately threaten the foundations of democracy. It is incumbent upon all of us, as informed citizens, to grapple with the implications of propaganda in our daily lives and to strive for greater awareness of the forces that seek to shape our perceptions.

As we conclude this examination of the psychological and ethical dimensions of propaganda, it is essential to reaffirm the importance of understanding the foundations of influence. Recognizing the psychological tactics that underpin propaganda, as well as the social dynamics that amplify its reach, empowers us to engage critically with the information we consume. It is through this empowerment that we can cultivate informed citizenship, challenging the narratives that seek to manipulate us and advocating for a more transparent and ethical discourse.

As we move forward into subsequent chapters, we will build upon this knowledge and look deeper into the ways in which propaganda continues to evolve in our modern world. The insights gained from understanding the psychological and ethical dimensions of propaganda will serve as a foundation upon which we can further explore the strategies employed by propagandists in contemporary society. In doing so, we will not only enhance our understanding of the mechanisms of influence but also fortify our resolve to engage responsibly with the information that shapes our lives and communities. The journey towards informed citizenship is ongoing, and it is one that requires vigilance, critical thinking, and a commitment to truth.

They're Lying to You

Chapter 2: Understanding Agenda-Setting in Media

In a world that bombards us with an endless stream of information, it often seems as though the news we consume is a reflection of the realities that surround us. Yet, those realities are not merely presented to us; they are carefully curated, sculpted, and presented through the lens of agenda-setting. Consider the 2016 United States presidential election, a pivotal moment in American politics that was dramatically influenced by the media. During this time, various media outlets framed the candidates and their policies in ways that significantly impacted public opinion, voter turnout, and ultimately, the election's outcome. For instance, the portrayal of certain issues—such as immigration, healthcare, and foreign policy—was heavily influenced by how these topics were covered by news networks and social media platforms.

When we analyze the media's role during this electoral cycle, it becomes clear that the topics emphasized by the press did not just inform the electorate; they actively shaped the public's perceptions and opinions on the candidates and their platforms. This phenomenon is encapsulated in the concept of agenda-setting, which posits that the media doesn't just tell us what to think about, but it also influences how we think about those issues. The media's power to highlight specific topics while downplaying others creates a framework through which the public engages with political discourse.

The roots of agenda-setting can be traced back to the seminal research conducted by Maxwell McCombs and Donald Shaw in the early 1970s. Their groundbreaking study during the 1968 presidential campaign revealed a striking correlation between the issues emphasized by the media and the issues that voters deemed important. They found that the topics covered most frequently by the press were the same ones that voters identified as pivotal to their decision-making processes. This key finding laid the foundation for agenda-setting theory, suggesting that the media plays a critical role in shaping public priorities.

Over the years, agenda-setting has evolved and expanded, encompassing various aspects of communication studies and social psychology. As we look deeper into this concept, it is essential to explore not only how the media sets the agenda but also the psychological mechanisms that influence our perceptions in this complex interplay between information and understanding.

To grasp the significance of agenda-setting, it is imperative to recognize the psychological mechanisms at play. Cognitive biases—systematic patterns of deviation from norm or rationality in judgment—serve as the catalysts that affect how individuals process information. Two particularly relevant biases in the context of agenda-setting are the availability heuristic and confirmation bias.

The availability heuristic is a mental shortcut that relies on immediate examples that come to mind when evaluating a specific topic, concept, method, or decision. In simpler terms, it means that if something can be recalled easily—like a sensational news story about crime or a viral video about social injustice—people are more likely to perceive it as important or more prevalent than it may actually be. When a media outlet extensively covers a particular incident, such as a high-profile criminal case or a natural disaster, it is likely that the audience will begin to see these events as more common or pressing concerns in their lives.

Confirmation bias, on the other hand, is the tendency to search for, interpret, favor, and recall information in a way that confirms one's preexisting beliefs or hypotheses. This means that when individuals are inundated with news, they are predisposed to accept information that aligns with their views while dismissing or undervaluing dissenting opinions. For example, during election cycles, voters who favor a particular candidate may seek out news articles, social media posts, or television segments that bolster their support, thus further reinforcing their beliefs and perceptions about the candidate and the issues at hand.

These cognitive biases do not operate in a vacuum; they are intricately linked to the media's agenda-setting function. When news outlets prioritize certain stories or angles over others, they effectively guide public attention toward particular issues, which in turn influences how people perceive their importance. During political campaigns, this influence can be particularly pronounced. For instance, media portrayals of candidates may leverage these biases, either emphasizing a candidate's strengths or highlighting their weaknesses depending on the narrative the media chooses to promote.

Take, for instance, the 2008 U.S. presidential election, where Barack Obama was often framed as a transformative figure capable of bringing about significant change, while his opponent, John McCain, was portrayed in a way that emphasized his connection to the status quo. The media's framing of these candidates not only shaped the public's perception of them but also sparked broader conversations about race, experience, and the future of the nation. As voters consumed this information, their biases and the media's agenda converged, ultimately influencing the election's outcome.

The power dynamics inherent in agenda-setting extend beyond individual voters, encompassing a diverse set of stakeholders, including political entities, corporations, and advocacy groups. Each of these actors possesses unique motivations and resources that they leverage to influence public discourse. Political parties, for example, often use media strategies to advance their agendas, framing issues in ways that resonate with their target demographics. Corporations may engage in similar tactics, utilizing public relations campaigns to shape perceptions of their products or practices. Advocacy groups harness the power of social media and traditional media to raise awareness about specific causes, hoping to sway public opinion and ultimately influence policy decisions.

Throughout history, the practice of agenda-setting has been evident in various contexts, particularly during wartime. Propaganda has been a powerful tool used to sway public sentiment, rally support for military endeavors, and vilify enemies. For example, during World War II, governments on both sides engaged in extensive propaganda campaigns to shape public perceptions of the war effort and the enemy. These campaigns often employed selective framing and emotional appeals to galvanize support and suppress dissent.

In the contemporary landscape, the rise of social media has transformed the dynamics of agenda-setting. Platforms such as Twitter and Facebook have given rise to new players in the media landscape—ordinary citizens, influencers, and grassroots organizations—who can set the agenda alongside traditional media outlets. The viral nature of online content allows issues to gain traction rapidly, often bypassing the gatekeeping functions of established media. The Black Lives Matter movement is a salient example of this phenomenon, illustrating how social media has become a powerful tool for raising awareness and shaping public discourse around issues of racial injustice and police brutality.

The interplay between traditional media, social media, and the various stakeholders involved in agenda-setting highlights the complexities of shaping public discourse. As we navigate this intricate web, it becomes clear that the process of agenda-setting is not merely about the dissemination of information; it is about power, influence, and the ongoing negotiation of meaning in a world awash in information.

In synthesizing these insights, we must acknowledge that the media serves not only as a conduit for information but as a fundamental architect of the public's understanding of critical issues. This raises profound questions about accountability, representation, and the ethical responsibilities of both journalists and consumers of news. As we move forward in this exploration of agenda-setting, it is crucial to examine the implications of these dynamics for democracy, civic engagement, and the future of public discourse in an increasingly fragmented media landscape.

As we reflect on the nature of agenda-setting, it invites us to consider our roles as both consumers and participants in the media ecosystem. With each article we read, each post we share, and each discussion we engage in, we are contributing to the ongoing dialogue that shapes public discourse. Understanding the mechanics behind agenda-setting empowers us to become more discerning consumers of media, encouraging us to question the narratives presented to us and to seek out diverse perspectives in an age of unprecedented information access.

In conclusion, the concept of agenda-setting serves as a critical lens through which we can view the media's influence on public perception and discourse. By unpacking the psychological mechanisms at play and recognizing the power dynamics involved, we can better understand the complexities of communication in our contemporary society. As we look deeper into the intricacies of agenda-setting, we will explore its implications for democracy, the role of new media in shaping narratives, and the responsibilities of both media producers and consumers in fostering informed public discourse. The journey ahead promises to unravel the multifaceted layers of agenda-setting, revealing the profound impact it has on our lives and the world around us.

In a world that is saturated with information, the ability to sift through the noise and determine what is relevant, credible, and impactful has never been more crucial. The media is not merely a passive conveyor of facts; it serves as an active participant in shaping public perception and discourse. This chapter looks into various case studies that illustrate the power of media in agenda-setting, followed by practical strategies for critical media consumption. By examining historical events alongside contemporary issues, we can uncover the methodologies employed by the media, while also equipping readers with the tools necessary to navigate this complex landscape effectively.

To begin with, we must look back at notable historical events, particularly the Watergate scandal, which serves as a quintessential example of media framing and its profound impact on public opinion. In the early 1970s, the Watergate scandal unfolded as a political drama that ultimately led to the resignation of President Richard Nixon. What began as a seemingly trivial break-in at the Democratic National Committee headquarters burgeoned into a sprawling investigation that exposed systemic corruption and abuse of power at the highest levels of government.

As the scandal unfolded, various media outlets played a pivotal role in shaping the narrative. The Washington Post, under the stewardship of journalists Bob Woodward and Carl Bernstein, made the courageous decision to pursue the story relentlessly, even in the face of intense pressure and threats. Their investigative reporting not only uncovered significant details about the scandal but also highlighted the broader issues of political accountability and ethical governance. The framing of Watergate by the media was instrumental in transforming it from a localized political mishap into a national crisis that demanded attention and action.

The agenda-setting role of the media became evident as public interest surged, leading to greater scrutiny of government actions. By focusing on the malfeasance of powerful individuals and the implications of their actions for democracy, the media was able to activate the public's sense of agency. This resulted in widespread public outcry, which ultimately compelled Congress to take action. The Watergate scandal underscores the profound impact media can have when it engages in principled journalism, serving as both an informant and a catalyst of change.

In examining contemporary issues, we can see a similar pattern of media influence, especially concerning climate change and social justice movements. The framing of climate change in recent years exemplifies how the media can elevate a scientific consensus into a pressing public issue that demands urgent action. Major news outlets have extensively covered the catastrophic consequences of climate change, showcasing extreme weather events, ecological degradation, and the voices of scientists advocating for immediate responses. This media framing has helped usher climate change from the sidelines of public discourse into the center of political and social agendas worldwide.

Moreover, social movements such as Black Lives Matter have also benefited from strategic media framing. The viral spread of the hashtag #BlackLivesMatter on social media platforms catalyzed a global movement against racial injustice and police brutality. Media coverage of protests, incidents of police violence, and personal stories of those impacted by systemic racism has not only brought these issues to light but has also shaped public perception and policy discussions around race, equity, and justice.

However, it is essential to recognize that not all attempts at agenda-setting are successful. For example, despite the extensive coverage of the opioid crisis, the framing of this issue within certain media outlets has sometimes failed to resonate with the broader public. The narrative has often focused on individual responsibility rather than systemic factors such as corporate greed and inadequate healthcare policies. This failure to adequately frame the issue could contribute to a lack of public urgency and action at the policy level.

As we proceed from these case studies, it becomes clear that the media plays a powerful role in shaping our understanding of the world. Yet, as consumers of media, we must approach what we read and see with a critical eye. It is not enough to merely absorb information; we must dissect media narratives to understand the underlying motivations and implications. Thus, it is crucial to equip ourselves with practical tools to navigate this complex terrain effectively.

Among the most powerful strategies for critical media consumption is the practice of cross-referencing sources. In an age where misinformation can spread like wildfire, it is imperative to verify the information we encounter. This involves checking multiple reputable sources to see how they report on the same story. By doing so, we can identify potential biases and discrepancies in reporting while gaining a more comprehensive understanding of the facts at hand. For instance, if an article claims a significant political event has taken place, verifying the information through other credible outlets will help us ascertain the accuracy of the claims.

Additionally, recognizing emotional appeals within media narratives is crucial. Media messages often employ emotional language and imagery to provoke a specific reaction from the audience. While emotional engagement can be a powerful tool for advocacy and awareness, it is essential to approach such narratives with a level of skepticism. Are the emotions elicited genuine reflections of the situation, or are they being strategically utilized to sway public opinion? By maintaining a critical perspective and asking these questions, consumers can avoid falling prey to sensationalism and manipulation.

Furthermore, understanding the role of framing in media messages allows for a deeper analysis of the information presented. Framing refers to the way information is organized and presented in a particular light, which can significantly influence public perception. For example, the framing of immigrants as "criminals" versus "refugees" can evoke vastly different emotional responses and public attitudes towards immigration policies. By being aware of the frames used in media narratives, we can better comprehend the motivations behind them and the potential implications for societal attitudes and policies.

As we conclude this exploration of case studies and practical strategies for critical media consumption, the importance of the informed citizen cannot be overstated. In an era where misinformation and media manipulation abound, active participation in public discourse is more vital than ever. Each individual has a responsibility to approach media critically, engage in discussions, and advocate for transparency and accountability within journalistic practices.

The call to action is clear: we must take charge of our media consumption. This involves not only developing critical media literacy skills but actively demanding more from our media outlets. We should advocate for journalism that is not only informative but also ethical and accountable. In our democratized society, the media serves as a powerful tool for both enlightenment and manipulation; thus, it is our duty as citizens to ensure that it fulfills its role as a bastion of truth and a platform for diverse voices.

In summary, the case studies of historical events like the Watergate scandal, alongside contemporary issues such as climate change and social justice movements, illustrate the intricate relationship between media and public discourse. The strategies for critical media consumption offer essential tools to dissect narratives, cross-reference information, and recognize emotional appeals. As we step into the future, the role of the informed citizen becomes paramount, as we strive for a media landscape that upholds integrity, transparency, and accountability. Only through proactive and engaged citizenship can we hope to cultivate a society that values truth, fosters informed debate, and champions the public good.

They're Lying to You

Chapter 3: The Psychological Foundations of Fear in Propaganda

Fear is a powerful psychological tool, one that has been harnessed throughout history to motivate, control, and influence behavior. In modern society, where the rapid flow of information can shape perceptions in a matter of seconds, fear-based messaging has become a staple in both political campaigns and advertising strategies. To understand the potency of fear as a weapon of persuasion, we begin with a compelling anecdote that encapsulates its profound impact.

Picture a bustling city on a seemingly ordinary day. Families go about their routines, children play in the parks, and commuters rush to their jobs. But as the sun begins to set, a news alert flashes across screens: "A stranger has been arrested for a series of violent crimes in your neighborhood." The report details a string of unsettling incidents, weaving a narrative of danger encroaching on the lives of unsuspecting residents. Within hours, social media is ablaze with discussions of safety, fear, and uncertainty. Community forums explode with worry as neighbors share tips on home security and vigilant parenting. The fabric of daily life is suddenly tinged with anxiety, a stark reminder of how fear can infiltrate our consciousness and dictate our actions.

This chapter will look into the psychological foundations of fear, exploring how it operates not only as an emotional response but also as a cognitive shaper of our worldviews. It will reveal the intricate ways in which fear influences decision-making, drives political agendas, and alters social dynamics. By dissecting the mechanisms behind fear-based messaging, we aim to illuminate why it remains a favored tactic in various forms of communication, particularly in the realms of politics and advertising.

Fear, at its core, is an instinctual response that has evolved through millennia of human experience. It triggers a biological reaction known as the fight-or-flight response, a mechanism that prepares the body to either confront danger or escape it. When faced with a perceived threat, the amygdala, a small almond-shaped structure in the brain, activates and signals the body to release adrenaline and cortisol. These hormones elevate heart rate, sharpen senses, and redirect energy to muscles, allowing for quick reactions. In this state, decision-making is often influenced by immediate emotional responses rather than rational thought processes. Thus, fear can heavily skew our judgment and prompt us to make choices that align more closely with self-preservation than with logical reasoning.

To better understand the role of fear in decision-making, we can look toward seminal psychological research. One critical study conducted by psychologists John D. Laird and David E. H. Hotchkiss utilized a pioneering technique known as "fear conditioning." In their experiments, they demonstrated how individuals could be conditioned to associate neutral stimuli with aversive events, leading to heightened fear responses. This research laid the groundwork for further investigations into how fear can shape behavior and cognition.

Subsequent studies have uncovered the staggering effects of fear on our psyche. For instance, research conducted by psychologists Paul Slovic and Ellen Peters revealed how fear can distort our perception of risk. Their work showed that when individuals are confronted with fear-inducing messages—such as warnings about the dangers of smoking or the threats posed by terrorism—they often overestimate the likelihood of these events occurring. In turn, this leads to irrational fears that can fuel anxiety and influence behaviors in ways that may not necessarily align with actual threats.

Fear is not merely a biological response; it is also deeply social and cultural. In political campaigns, fear is a strategic asset leveraged to mobilize voters, shape opinions, and sway public sentiment. Politicians and political strategists have long understood that fear can be an effective tool for galvanizing support and rallying opposition. For instance, during election seasons, candidates may emphasize the dangers of crime, immigration, or terrorism to create a sense of urgency among voters. They craft narratives that frame their opponents as threats to safety and stability, thereby positioning themselves as the protectors who will fend off these dangers.

Case studies in political history reveal the effectiveness of fear appeals. Take, for example, the infamous "Willie Horton" ad campaign during the 1988 presidential election. The advertisement highlighted the story of a convicted felon, Willie Horton, who committed a violent crime while on furlough from a Massachusetts prison. The ad branded then-Governor Michael Dukakis as soft on crime and portrayed him as a direct threat to public safety. This chilling message resonated with voters, contributing to George H.W. Bush's victory in that election. The Horton case illustrates the power of fear-based messaging to influence political outcomes, emphasizing how fear can be weaponized against opponents.

In the realm of public health, fear is similarly employed to provoke action. Consider the stark warnings issued during the COVID-19 pandemic; health organizations utilized fear-driven campaigns to communicate the virus's severity and the necessity of preventive measures. Images of overwhelmed hospitals, graphic statistics on mortality rates, and personal testimonies from those who suffered from the virus created a compelling narrative that demanded attention. The messages were designed not only to inform but also to instill fear, prompting individuals to comply with public health guidelines such as mask-wearing and social distancing.

Techniques used in fear-based messaging are often characterized by vivid imagery, emotional storytelling, and selective statistics. For instance, a public service announcement might juxtapose bright, cheerful images of family gatherings with stark, black-and-white visuals of empty hospital beds to evoke a sense of loss and urgency. The emotional weight of such contrasts serves to heighten fear and compel the audience to take action. Emotional storytelling, too, plays a crucial role in fear messaging. By weaving personal narratives into broader issues, communicators can create relatable and poignant experiences that resonate with audiences, driving home the message that fear must be acknowledged and addressed.

Moreover, the careful selection of statistics can amplify fear's impact. By emphasizing particular data points while omitting context, communicators can create a distorted perception of reality. For example, citing the number of violent crimes in a city without considering the overall crime rate can lead to an exaggerated sense of danger. This selective use of information can manipulate public perception and behavior, leading to increased fear and subsequent action— whether it be voting for a tough-on-crime candidate or supporting draconian public safety measures.

While the efficacy of fear-based messaging is well-documented, it is essential to consider the ethical implications of using fear as a communication tool. The question arises: when, if ever, is it justifiable to leverage fear to influence behavior? The ethical landscape of fear-based propaganda is fraught with dilemmas. On one hand, communicators may argue that fear can lead to positive outcomes, such as increased awareness of public health issues or enhanced community safety measures. On the other hand, there is a risk that fear can incite panic, exacerbate social divisions, and lead to harmful consequences.

One of the ethical challenges of fear-based messaging is the potential to manipulate emotions without regard for the truth. When fear is used to drive narratives, it can lead to sensationalism, misrepresentation, and a breakdown of trust. Audiences may become desensitized to fear over time, leading to apathy or skepticism toward legitimate threats. This erosion of trust can undermine public discourse, making it difficult to engage in constructive conversations about important issues.

Furthermore, ethical considerations must also account for the target audience's vulnerability. Fear-based messaging can disproportionately affect marginalized groups, who may already experience heightened levels of anxiety and insecurity. For instance, campaigns that stoke fears about immigration can perpetuate harmful stereotypes and contribute to a culture of hostility and exclusion. When fear is weaponized in this manner, it can have devastating effects on communities and relationships.

As we navigate the complex terrain of fear in propaganda, it is crucial to recognize the thin line between persuasion and manipulation. While fear can motivate individuals to take action, it is essential to consider the broader implications of such tactics. Are we fostering a culture of fear and division, or are we encouraging informed and empathetic responses to societal challenges? Ultimately, the ends do not always justify the means, and as communicators, we bear a responsibility to engage with our audiences in ways that prioritize truth, compassion, and understanding.

In conclusion, this exploration of the psychological foundations of fear in propaganda reveals both the power and ethical quandaries of fear as a tool for persuasion. Through historical examples and psychological insights, we see how fear can mobilize action, shape political landscapes, and influence public behavior. Yet, with this power comes a responsibility to wield fear ethically, recognizing its potential to harm as well as to inform. As we move forward, it is imperative to critically assess how fear is used in our communication and to strive for narratives that uplift rather than diminish the human experience.

In the intricate web of communication that permeates our daily lives, the phenomenon of fear-mongering stands out like a chilling specter, casting shadows over reason and clarity. Fear-mongering, at its core, is a strategy that leverages fear—often exaggerated or unfounded—to manipulate individuals and societies into certain actions or beliefs. This tactic is deeply embedded in media narratives, where the allure of heightened emotions often outweighs the responsibility of providing balanced and factual reporting. The prevalence of fear-mongering in contemporary society is alarming; it has become a tool wielded not just by sensationalist news outlets, but also by politicians, marketers, and various social forces seeking to sway public opinion.

The media landscape today is riddled with sensationalism, where the pursuit of audience engagement frequently eclipses journalistic integrity. For instance, during the COVID-19 pandemic, news coverage often focused on the starkest, most dramatic developments—

overwhelmed hospitals, rising death tolls, and dire predictions—while marginalized discussions around recovery rates, resilience, and community support. Such narratives create an environment where fear thrives, feeding into a cycle of anxiety that affects individual behavior and societal cohesion. The tendency to amplify societal fears has profound implications, altering the public's perception of reality and leading to a heightened sense of insecurity. This critical analysis of sensationalist news coverage is essential in understanding how fear-mongering operates and the profound effects it can have on our collective psyche.

A plethora of case studies illustrates the pernicious nature of fear-mongering, particularly in the context of the COVID-19 pandemic. From the initial outbreak, when reports emerged of a mysterious virus wreaking havoc in distant lands, media narratives often skewed towards the terrifying potential of the virus. As the situation escalated, fear-based messaging became even more prevalent: headlines screamed of impending doom, while images of empty streets and overflowing hospitals dominated our screens. This constant barrage of alarming information not only heightened public anxiety but also distorted the perception of risk.

The impact of this fear was palpable in the behavior of individuals and communities. Panic buying, for instance, swept through supermarkets as people prepared for an uncertain future, driven by the belief that supplies would dwindle. Social distancing measures were sometimes met with resistance as fear of the unknown clashed with a profound desire for normalcy. In many instances, the media's portrayal of the virus as an omnipresent threat overshadowed the nuanced discussions around effective coping strategies, community resilience, and the importance of mental health during such trying times.

Analyzing how fear has been leveraged in media narratives reveals a troubling trend: the tendency to prioritize sensationalism over responsible reporting. When fear becomes a tool for engagement, it contributes to a distorted understanding of reality and fuels societal divisions. Those in positions of power and influence have at times manipulated this fear for their gain, framing narratives that serve their interests while disregarding the broader implications for public health and safety. This exploitation of fear highlights the urgent need for critical engagement with the media, encouraging individuals to question the motives behind the messaging they encounter.

To navigate the treacherous waters of fear-based messaging, it is imperative to cultivate an acute awareness of the techniques used to recognize fear-mongering. Practical strategies can empower individuals to identify these tactics and resist their influence. Among the most effective strategies is the practice of questioning the sources of information. Who is delivering the message? What are their motives? Understanding the background and intent of the source can provide crucial context that informs our interpretation of the information presented.

Additionally, recognizing emotional triggers is essential in identifying fear-based manipulation. Fear mongers often exploit our innate responses to danger, crafting narratives that evoke visceral reactions. By developing the ability to discern when a message is designed to elicit fear rather than reasoned discussion, individuals can begin to distance themselves from fear-based narratives. A checklist of indicators can serve as a useful tool: Are there exaggerated claims? Is there a lack of balanced perspectives? Are emotional appeals prioritized over factual evidence? If the answers lean towards the affirmative, it is likely that fear is being utilized as a manipulative device.

Another vital technique for resisting fear-based propaganda involves seeking balanced perspectives. Engaging with a variety of sources and viewpoints allows individuals to construct a more comprehensive understanding of complex issues. By diversifying our media consumption, we can counteract the myopic narratives that often dominate mainstream discourse. This practice not only fosters informed opinions but also nurtures critical thinking skills that are essential for navigating an increasingly polarized world.

Cultivating resilience against fear-based messaging is not merely about recognizing tactics; it also involves fostering a mindset that values education and awareness over sensationalism. Encouragement is crucial here, as individuals are invited to explore the depths of their consciousness, to confront their fears, and to challenge the narratives that seek to manipulate them. By promoting conversations around media literacy and critical thinking within communities, we can arm ourselves and others against the pervasive influence of fear-mongering.

In summary, the significance of recognizing and countering fear-mongering cannot be overstated. The analysis of fear-based media narratives, the examination of case studies, and the exploration of practical strategies all culminate in a powerful call to action. As we reflect on the key points discussed, it becomes apparent that the responsibility to promote awareness and critical thinking lies within each of us. By committing to challenge fear-based propaganda and fostering open dialogue in our communities, we can contribute to a more informed and resilient society.

The journey forward requires us to embrace education and self-awareness as bulwarks against manipulation. As we confront the realities of fear in our media, we must also remember that we hold the power to question, to analyze, and to resist the darker impulses of fear-mongering. In doing so, we not only uphold democratic values but also empower ourselves and those around us to navigate an increasingly complex world with clarity and confidence. Together, we can build a collective resistance against fear-based narratives, fostering a culture that prioritizes understanding and solidarity over division and anxiety.

Chapter 4: The Nature of Societal Biases and Their Exploitation by Propaganda

In the intricate tapestry of human society, biases are like threads—woven in a myriad of patterns that reflect our collective experiences, cultural narratives, and historical legacies. At their core, societal biases are the mental shortcuts and preconceptions that shape our perceptions, judgments, and interactions with one another. These biases can manifest in a multitude of ways, influencing everything from individual decision-making to the broader societal norms that govern behaviors and attitudes. They are often deeply embedded within cultural contexts, molded by historical experiences, socialization processes, and collective memory.

To define societal bias is to look into the realm of cognitive psychology, which provides us with the tools to unpack how these biases arise and persist. Biases are not inherently negative; they are often subconscious shortcuts that allow individuals to navigate the complexities of life without becoming overwhelmed. However, when left unchecked, these biases can lead to flawed reasoning, unfair judgments, and ultimately, societal divisions.

Cognitive dissonance, a concept introduced by Leon Festinger in the 1950s, refers to the mental discomfort experienced when one's beliefs are challenged by new information or experiences. This discomfort often leads individuals to ignore, dismiss, or rationalize conflicting evidence in order to maintain their existing beliefs. In the realm of societal biases, cognitive dissonance plays a crucial role as it can perpetuate stereotypes and cultural norms, making it difficult for people to embrace alternative perspectives.

Confirmation bias, on the other hand, is the tendency for individuals to seek out and give greater weight to information that confirms their existing beliefs while ignoring or discounting information that contradicts them. This phenomenon is particularly potent in the context of societal biases, as it reinforces pre-existing stereotypes and can lead to a self-fulfilling prophecy where the biased beliefs become ingrained and further entrenched within a community or culture. Together, cognitive dissonance and confirmation bias create a powerful mechanism that maintains the status quo of societal biases, often resisting change and perpetuating harmful narratives.

To understand the full impact of these biases, we must explore their historical context, particularly how they have been exploited through propaganda. Throughout history, propaganda has served as a tool for shaping public opinion, often leveraging societal biases to achieve specific objectives. A notable example of this can be found in the lead-up to World War II, a period marked by intense nationalistic fervor and deep-seated biases that would be capitalized upon by various governments.

During this tumultuous time, propaganda took many forms—posters, speeches, films, and more—each designed to evoke emotions, manipulate perceptions, and galvanize support for the war effort. The narrative woven through these propaganda pieces was often steeped in cultural stereotypes, portraying enemy nations in dehumanizing ways that justified aggression and fostered a sense of superiority among the populace.

One of the most striking examples of this can be seen in the propaganda disseminated by Nazi Germany. Posters depicting Jewish individuals as vermin or rats served to dehumanize an entire population, reducing them to mere pests that needed to be eradicated. These images did not exist in a vacuum; they were the culmination of centuries of anti-Semitic sentiment, which had been perpetuated through societal biases that painted Jewish people as outsiders, untrustworthy and malevolent.

Similarly, British and American propaganda depicted the German enemy as barbaric, often utilizing caricatures that exaggerated negative traits, reinforcing stereotypes of the "savage" German soldier. These portrayals, steeped in a sense of cultural superiority, were designed to unify the home front by fostering a shared enemy, thus leveraging societal biases to promote a sense of purpose and determination.

Films of the era, such as "Why We Fight," produced by the United States government, further exemplified how propaganda exploited societal biases. These films aimed to justify American involvement in the war, using imagery and narratives that appealed to the public's sense of duty, morality, and national pride. They painted a stark contrast between the perceived virtues of democracy and the supposed vices of totalitarian regimes, reinforcing existing biases while fostering a moral imperative to engage in conflict.

As we transition into the contemporary landscape, it becomes clear that the mechanisms of propaganda have evolved, yet the exploitation of societal biases remains a potent tool in the arsenal of political and social influence. The rise of social media has transformed the way information is disseminated, allowing for the rapid spread of narratives that can amplify pre-existing biases and deepen societal divides.

Modern political campaigns have increasingly harnessed the power of social media platforms to target specific demographics with tailored messages that resonate with their existing beliefs. Algorithms designed to maximize user engagement often prioritize sensational content that elicits strong emotional responses, creating an environment where divisive narratives can thrive. This not only reinforces confirmation bias among users but also creates echo chambers— spaces where individuals are insulated from opposing viewpoints, further entrenching their biases.

Moreover, the proliferation of misinformation has emerged as a formidable challenge in contemporary society. False narratives, often propagated through social media, have the potential to distort public perception and entrench societal biases. In times of crisis, misinformation can spread like wildfire, exacerbating fears and prejudices, as seen during the COVID-19 pandemic with the scapegoating of certain communities and the propagation of conspiracy theories.

The implications of these contemporary manifestations of propaganda are profound. The manipulation of societal biases through modern media not only shapes public opinion but can also influence policy decisions, electoral outcomes, and societal cohesion. As individuals become increasingly susceptible to the allure of narratives that confirm their biases, the fabric of society risks unraveling, leading to polarization and conflict.

In conclusion, the interplay between societal biases and propaganda is both complex and significant. From historical examples of wartime propaganda that weaponized cultural stereotypes to contemporary political campaigns that exploit social media algorithms, the tactics may have evolved, but the underlying principles remain largely unchanged. It is imperative for individuals and societies alike to cultivate critical thinking skills, challenge their biases, and seek out diverse perspectives to mitigate the insidious effects of propaganda. Only through a conscious effort to confront and transcend our biases can we hope to foster a more informed and cohesive society, one that values understanding over division and empathy over animosity.

In the contemporary landscape of information consumption, where narratives often clash and polarization reigns, it becomes imperative to equip ourselves with the tools necessary for recognizing and addressing both personal and societal biases. The ability to engage critically with information demands not only a fundamental understanding of our own predispositions but also a willingness to confront the structures and cultural norms that shape our perspectives. As we explore the methods for overcoming biases, we embark on a journey that calls for introspection, analytical rigor, and a commitment to informed and equitable discourse.

To begin, recognizing biases—both personal and societal—requires an acute awareness of the lens through which we view the world. Biases often manifest subtly, woven into the fabric of our thoughts and beliefs by the societal narratives we absorb from various sources: media, education, and cultural heritage. These biases can skew our perception of reality, leading us to filter information in a way that reinforces our existing beliefs instead of challenging them.

One effective method for identifying personal biases is through reflective questioning. By examining our own viewpoints, we can uncover the assumptions that underpin them. For instance, when confronted with a controversial issue, we can ask ourselves, "What prior experiences or influences led me to this conclusion?" or "Am I considering alternative perspectives, or am I merely seeking confirmation of my beliefs?" Such questions not only elucidate our biases but also encourage a more open-minded exploration of the various facets of an issue.

Moreover, critical thinking frameworks, such as the Paul-Elder model, provide structured approaches to evaluating information. This model emphasizes the importance of clarity, accuracy, relevance, depth, breadth, logic, significance, and fairness in our analysis. Utilizing these criteria, we can dissect arguments, identify flaws in reasoning, and assess the credibility of sources. For example, when engaging with a news article or opinion piece, we can evaluate not just the content but also the sources cited, the context in which the information is presented, and the potential motivations behind the author's perspective.

Yet, it is not enough to merely recognize biases; we must actively challenge them. This is where cultivating a questioning mindset becomes essential. Embracing skepticism does not imply dismissing all information as false or misleading; rather, it entails approaching information with curiosity and an openness to multiple viewpoints. We should aspire to ask probing questions: "What might I be missing?" or "How might this perspective change if viewed through a different cultural or ideological lens?" Such inquiries can lead to richer understanding and diminish the likelihood of falling prey to confirmation bias.

In addition to fostering an inquisitive mindset, promoting constructive dialogue is vital for bridging divides within our communities. Engaging with individuals who hold contrasting views can often be daunting, yet it is through dialogue that we can expand our horizons and deepen our understanding of complex issues. To effectively communicate across differing perspectives, it is crucial to adopt an approach that prioritizes respect, empathy, and active listening.

One tip for engaging in constructive dialogue is to focus on shared values rather than differences. By identifying common ground, participants can create a foundation of mutual respect from which to explore divergent viewpoints. For instance, when discussing contentious topics such as climate change or immigration, one might begin by acknowledging a shared commitment to community well-being or the desire for a sustainable future. This emphasis on shared goals establishes a collaborative atmosphere, encouraging openness and reducing defensiveness.

Furthermore, employing active listening techniques can significantly enhance the quality of dialogue. This involves giving full attention to the speaker, demonstrating genuine interest in their perspective, and refraining from interrupting. Paraphrasing what the other person has said can also be an effective method of ensuring understanding and validating their viewpoint. When individuals feel heard and respected, they are more likely to reciprocate the same level of engagement, promoting a constructive exchange of ideas.

Another powerful strategy for fostering understanding across divides is to employ empathy as a guiding principle. This means striving to understand not only what others believe but also why they hold those beliefs. By seeking to comprehend the emotional and experiential factors that shape a person's perspective, we can move beyond surface-level disagreements and engage with the underlying reasons that fuel differing opinions. Empathy does not necessitate agreement; rather, it invites us to acknowledge the humanity in others and recognize that their experiences are valid, even if they differ from our own.

As we empower ourselves to engage critically with information and promote constructive dialogue, we must also recognize that this process is not merely an academic exercise—it is a call to action. Vigilance in information consumption and dialogue is essential in a world where misinformation proliferates and societal biases are deeply entrenched.

In this context, it is imperative for readers to realize their role as informed citizens. This involves actively seeking out diverse viewpoints, challenging their own biases, and remaining open to new information that may disrupt their preconceived notions. It is a commitment to being engaged participants in the democratic process, where discourse thrives on the basis of respect and equity.

Moreover, striving for equitable discourse transcends the mere act of talking; it is about creating spaces where all voices are heard and valued. This requires us to be vigilant in our interactions, ensuring that marginalized perspectives are not overlooked or silenced. By amplifying underrepresented voices and acknowledging the disparities that exist within societal narratives, we cultivate an environment conducive to genuine understanding and collaboration.

Recognizing our biases is also crucial in understanding the techniques employed in propaganda. Propaganda often exploits cognitive biases, manipulating information to evoke emotional responses rather than informed thought. By familiarizing ourselves with these techniques, we can better navigate the complexities of information consumption and resist the allure of sensationalism. For example, understanding the role of confirmation bias can empower individuals to question the validity of emotionally charged narratives that align with their pre-existing beliefs.

As we strive for informed citizenship, it becomes essential to foster a culture of critical engagement. This culture is built on the premise that questioning is not an act of defiance but rather an essential aspect of growth and understanding. Encouraging others to embrace this mindset can create ripple effects within our communities, leading to more informed discussions that transcend surface-level disagreements.

In conclusion, overcoming biases and engaging critically with information is a multifaceted endeavor that requires dedication and intentionality. By recognizing and addressing societal biases, promoting constructive dialogue, and empowering ourselves to act with vigilance, we can cultivate an environment that fosters informed citizenship and equitable discourse. As we navigate the complexities of contemporary society, let us remain committed to the pursuit of understanding, empathy, and respect, creating a more inclusive narrative that embraces the richness of diverse perspectives. This journey may be challenging, yet it is a necessary path toward a more informed and cohesive society. In this age of information, let us be not only consumers of knowledge but also active participants in the discourse that shapes our collective understanding of the world.

They're Lying to You

Chapter 5: Riding the Wave of Success

The concept of success is often accompanied by a multitude of strategies, narratives, and persuasive techniques, all aimed at consolidating and promoting a particular vision of the future. One such technique that has woven itself into the fabric of our public discourse is the "inevitable victory" propaganda technique. This subchapter aims to dissect this powerful narrative device, uncovering its definition, psychological underpinnings, and far-reaching implications.

The "inevitable victory" propaganda technique is a rhetorical strategy that paints the picture of a particular outcome as not merely desirable but as an unavoidable reality. It suggests that success is not just possible, but rather, it is predetermined—a fait accompli waiting to happen. This technique operates on the premise that if enough people believe in the certainty of an outcome, it can manifest into existence. As such, it plays a pivotal role in shaping public perception, influencing decision-making, and ultimately steering the course of events.

At its core, the inevitable victory technique seeks to create a sense of momentum around an idea, a candidate, a movement, or a product. By positing that success is guaranteed, it cultivates an environment where doubts are discouraged, and the status quo is challenged less frequently. In this context, rhetoric becomes a tool of empowerment, or conversely, a mechanism of control, often blurring the lines between inspiration and manipulation.

To grasp the magnitude of the inevitable victory technique, it is essential to explore its psychological underpinnings. One of the most compelling concepts that underlies this technique is the bandwagon effect. The bandwagon effect refers to the phenomenon where people are more likely to adopt a belief or take action because they perceive that others are doing the same. This social influence creates a ripple effect, whereby the more individuals that jump on the bandwagon, the more others are inclined to follow suit—believing that if everyone else is doing it, there must be some truth to it.

In this way, the inevitable victory narrative feeds into the bandwagon effect, reinforcing the notion that success is not only likely but is, in fact, already happening. As more individuals become convinced of this perceived inevitability, a collective mindset emerges, making it increasingly difficult for dissenters to voice their concerns or alternative viewpoints. The narrative itself can gain a life of its own, reinforced not by an objective analysis of facts, but by the sheer volume of belief and enthusiasm surrounding it.

Adding another layer of complexity to this phenomenon is the impact of social proof. Social proof serves as a psychological mechanism whereby individuals look to the behavior of others to guide their own actions and beliefs. This is particularly relevant in today's world, where social media has become a dominant force in shaping perceptions and opinions.

Social media platforms facilitate the rapid dissemination of information and opinions, creating echo chambers where certain narratives can thrive unchallenged. Within these spaces, the inevitable victory narrative can easily gain traction, as individuals are bombarded with positive affirmations and testimonials from others who have adopted the same belief. This amplification serves not only to solidify the narrative but also to ostracize those who dare to question the prevailing wisdom. Those who dissent may find themselves marginalized, their voices drowned out by the cacophony of collective agreement.

The ramifications of the inevitable victory technique extend far beyond mere social dynamics; they can profoundly influence the political landscape and the functioning of democratic systems. When a particular ideology or political figure is framed as invincible, it creates a discouraging environment for critical analysis and dissent. Individuals may feel compelled to support a candidate or policy simply because it is portrayed as the "winning" choice, rather than engaging with the underlying principles and potential consequences of their support.

Furthermore, the dangers associated with the inevitable victory technique can manifest in forms of complacency and blind obedience. When individuals believe that a certain outcome is guaranteed, they may become less vigilant or engaged in the democratic process. This disengagement can lead to a lack of accountability, as those in power may feel less pressured to address the concerns of their constituents, believing that their victory is assured regardless of their actions.

In democratic contexts, where the health of the system relies on active participation and informed debate, the complacency fostered by the inevitable victory narrative can be particularly detrimental. It can create a cycle where citizens no longer feel the need to engage critically with their leaders or hold them accountable, resulting in a dangerous erosion of democratic values.

As we unpack the layers of the inevitable victory technique, it becomes clear that while it may initially appear to be a tool for galvanizing support and fostering optimism, its implications are far-reaching and complex. The delicate balance between inspiring hope and fostering blind allegiance must be navigated with care, for the very essence of democracy thrives on informed dissent, critical inquiry, and the active engagement of its citizens.

The complex interplay between the inevitable victory technique, the bandwagon effect, and the mechanisms of social proof all contribute to a cultural landscape where dissent can be stifled and critical thinking undermined. As we continue to explore this fascinating yet troubling dynamic, it is essential to remain vigilant in our commitment to fostering a discourse that values diverse perspectives, critical engagement, and an unwavering pursuit of truth. Only then can we truly ride the wave of success without succumbing to the pitfalls of complacency and blind allegiance that the inevitable victory technique so easily entices us to embrace.

By understanding the mechanisms at play behind this technique, we equip ourselves with the tools necessary to navigate the complexities of contemporary discourse. We must remain ever-aware of the narratives that shape our perceptions, always questioning and seeking to understand the underlying motivations and implications of the ideas we encounter.

In this age of information overload and rapid-fire communication, the responsibility lies with each individual to critically engage with the narratives that permeate our social landscapes. By doing so, we can ensure that we do not merely become passive participants in a chorus of unquestioned beliefs but rather active agents in crafting a future defined by informed choices and empowered voices.

The journey toward understanding the inevitable victory technique is not merely an academic exercise; it is a crucial step in fostering a more resilient and informed society. In a world where narratives can sway opinions and shape destinies, it is imperative that we cultivate a culture of critical thought, where every voice is valued and every perspective considered. This is how we can truly ride the wave of success, ensuring that it is a wave driven by conviction, understanding, and a commitment to the ideals that uphold our shared humanity.

As we draw to a close on this exploration, let us carry forward the insights gleaned about the inevitable victory technique, employing them as a lens through which to view the world around us. In doing so, we can navigate the complexities of modern discourse with a discerning eye, fostering an environment where truth, accountability, and engagement flourish.

In conclusion, the inevitable victory technique stands as a testament to the power of narrative in shaping belief systems and societal dynamics. It serves as both a mirror reflecting our collective aspirations and a lens through which we can scrutinize the motivations behind the narratives that seek to shape our reality. As we continue to look deeper into the complexities of human behavior and societal trends, let us remain committed to fostering a narrative landscape that celebrates critical thought, embraces diverse perspectives, and champions the ideals of democracy and human rights.

The path toward genuine understanding and engagement may not always be straightforward, but it is a path worth traversing—one that can lead us toward a more informed and enlightened society, where every voice matters, and every opinion is heard. In this journey, the Inevitable Victory Technique serves as a powerful reminder of the responsibilities we bear as participants in the collective narrative of our time. Let us rise to that challenge, embracing the task of not only understanding the techniques that shape our perceptions but also actively engaging in the creation of narratives that inspire hope, encourage critical inquiry, and promote a future defined by success in its most meaningful sense.

In the intricate landscape of modern political campaigning and social movements, one cannot underestimate the profound impact of narrative. Narratives shape perceptions, motivate action, and often dictate the course of events. At the heart of many successful movements and campaigns lies a potent technique: the narrative of inevitable victory. This technique, when effectively employed, can energize a base, mobilize supporters, and create a compelling vision for the future that resonates deeply within the hearts and minds of the populace. This chapter looks into case studies that exemplify the application of this narrative in political campaigns and social movements, illustrating both its power and its implications.

The 2008 presidential campaign of Barack Obama stands as a remarkable testament to the effective utilization of the inevitable victory narrative. As he emerged as the Democratic frontrunner against a crowded field, Obama's campaign crafted a storyline that not only captured the imagination of supporters but also framed his candidacy as a historical movement. This crafted narrative suggested that progress was not merely possible, but inevitable—a promise that sparked hope and enthusiasm among millions. The campaign characterized Obama's candidacy as a transformative moment in American history, one that would usher in a new era of change, unity, and progress.

Throughout the campaign, Obama's team adeptly harnessed the power of language and imagery, presenting his vision as not just a campaign, but a movement reminiscent of the civil rights struggle and other pivotal moments in American history. This framing elicited a powerful emotional response from voters, fostering a sense of urgency and belonging. The narrative positioned Obama as not only a candidate but a vessel for the collective aspirations of a diverse electorate. By presenting his candidacy through this lens, the campaign instilled a belief in the inevitability of victory that transcended traditional political boundaries, engaging not only the base of the Democratic Party but also disaffected voters who had grown disillusioned with the status quo.

One of the most striking aspects of the 2008 campaign was how it mobilized a vast array of supporters, particularly young voters who were drawn to the optimistic vision of the future that Obama represented. His slogan, "Yes We Can," became a rallying cry that encapsulated the essence of the inevitable victory narrative. The campaign effectively positioned a vote for Obama as a vote for change—not just in leadership, but in the very fabric of American society. This narrative was instrumental in energizing the base and translating enthusiasm into tangible political action, leading to an unprecedented turnout on Election Day.

Moreover, the Obama campaign leveraged innovative strategies to amplify this narrative, including a robust social media presence that allowed for direct engagement with supporters. Platforms

like Facebook and Twitter became
essential tools for spreading the message
of inevitable victory. The campaign
cultivated a sense of community and
belonging among supporters, fostering a
belief that they were part of something
larger—an unstoppable movement that
would reshape the nation. The narrative of
inevitable victory, thus, became a self-
fulfilling prophecy; as more individuals
joined the cause, the belief in its success
grew stronger, creating a virtuous cycle
that propelled the campaign forward.

As the campaign progressed, the
sense of momentum built upon itself.
Media coverage often framed Obama's
candidacy as the inevitable choice, with
pundits speculating on the profound
implications of his potential presidency.
This perception of inevitability was further
reinforced by key endorsements from
prominent figures and organizations,
creating an additional layer of validation
for supporters. The narrative of historical
significance became intertwined with the
very act of voting for Obama,
transforming an electoral decision into a
moral imperative. The campaign's
portrayal of the candidacy as a historical

movement not only energized supporters but also led to increased public participation, as more individuals felt compelled to engage in the political process.

Turning our focus to a different realm of social change, the 2011 Arab Spring movements provide a vivid illustration of the role of narrative in shaping public perception. The collective unrest that swept across the Middle East and North Africa was marked by a palpable sense of hope and the belief in the inevitability of change. In countries like Tunisia and Egypt, citizens took to the streets, emboldened by a narrative that suggested their struggles would lead to liberation from oppressive regimes. The Arab Spring became synonymous with the belief that a new era of democracy and freedom was not just desirable, but within reach.

Social media played a pivotal role in this narrative construction, acting as a catalyst for mobilization and a platform for disseminating messages of hope. The ability to share stories, images, and videos in real-time allowed activists to create a sense of solidarity and shared purpose.

Hashtags like #Jan25, which referred to the protests in Egypt, became rallying calls for individuals seeking change. The narrative of inevitable success was amplified through these digital platforms, fostering a belief among citizens that they were part of a larger, unstoppable wave of transformation.

The initial successes of the Arab Spring reinforced this narrative of inevitable change. In Tunisia, the ousting of President Zine El Abidine Ben Ali was seen as a victory that validated the aspirations of protesters and inspired similar uprisings across the region. This early momentum contributed to a collective belief that further successes were not only possible but likely. Demonstrations erupted in countries such as Libya, Yemen, and Syria, as citizens rallied under the banner of freedom and social justice. The widespread belief in the inevitability of success created a powerful psychological effect, galvanizing individuals to act in pursuit of a brighter future.

However, the aftermath of these movements serves as a poignant reminder that the narrative of inevitable victory can be both empowering and misleading. While the initial enthusiasm and optimism were palpable, many of the subsequent uprisings faced significant challenges. The complexities of political transition, coupled with the realities of entrenched power structures, led to a cycle of disillusionment in several nations. As the narrative of inevitable success clashed with the harsh realities of political strife, many citizens grappled with the consequences of their hope.

In reflecting on these two case studies—Obama's 2008 presidential campaign and the Arab Spring movements—we unearth several key takeaways regarding the application of the inevitable victory narrative. First and foremost, it's evident that narratives wield immense power in shaping public perception and mobilizing support. The ability to craft a compelling story that resonates on an emotional level can foster a sense of urgency, belonging, and shared purpose among individuals. This storytelling aspect is paramount in both political contexts and social movements, as it can inspire action and reshape societal dynamics.

Moreover, the interplay between narrative and social media cannot be overstated. In an era defined by digital communication, the capacity to spread a message quickly and effectively amplifies the potential for collective action. Social media platforms serve as catalysts for movements, enabling individuals to connect, share experiences, and reinforce the belief in the possibility of change. The Arab Spring exemplified how digital tools could galvanize a populace and foster a sense of shared destiny, while Obama's campaign showcased the importance of narrative in translating that belief into electoral success.

However, it is essential to approach these narratives with a critical lens. While the allure of an inevitable victory can be intoxicating, it is crucial to recognize the complexities and challenges that often accompany movements for change. The enthusiasm generated by a compelling narrative can sometimes overshadow the practical realities of political engagement, leading to disillusionment when expectations are not met. Consequently, it is vital for individuals to remain engaged, informed, and critical of the narratives they encounter, questioning the underlying motivations and potential consequences of the stories being told.

As readers reflect on these dynamics, consider your own experiences with the narratives that have shaped your beliefs and actions. Have you ever been drawn into a movement or campaign by the promise of inevitable victory? What were the implications of that belief on your engagement with the cause? These questions invite a deeper exploration of the persuasive narratives that permeate our society, encouraging a more nuanced understanding of their role in shaping our reality.

In conclusion, the inevitable victory narrative is a powerful tool that has been employed in both political campaigns and social movements to inspire action and shape public perception. While its capacity to energize and mobilize supporters is undeniable, it is essential to remain critically engaged with the narratives we encounter. The stories we tell and believe in have the power to shape not only our perceptions but also the course of history. As we navigate a world filled with persuasive narratives, let us approach them with a discerning eye, recognizing the potential for change while remaining mindful of the complexities that lie ahead.

Chapter 6: The Psychology of Influence

Understanding Social
Proof and Its Psychological Mechanisms
Social proof, in its essence, refers
to the phenomenon wherein individuals
look to the behavior of others to inform
their own actions, especially in situations
of uncertainty. This foundational concept
is prevalent in various aspects of daily life,
from the seemingly trivial choices we
make – such as which restaurant to dine in
– to more significant life decisions, such as
career paths and political affiliations. The
relevance of social proof in decision-
making cannot be overstated, as it often
serves as a guiding beacon in the murky
waters of social interactions and
contextual ambiguity.

Consider, for instance, a bustling
city street on a Saturday evening, alive
with the sounds of laughter, clinking
glasses, and the tantalizing aroma of
diverse cuisines wafting through the air.
Imagine walking along this street, your
stomach rumbling and your mind racing

with hunger. You pass by several restaurants, some with empty tables and others with a line of eager patrons snaking out the door. The decision seems straightforward. You instinctively gravitate towards the restaurant with the crowd, assuming that the presence of so many diners is a testament to the quality of food and service within. Upon entering, you find yourself enveloped in a vibrant atmosphere, affirming your choice was indeed correct. This is social proof in action – a subtle psychological mechanism that guides our decisions based on the collective behavior of others.

Delving deeper into the psychological foundations that underpin social proof reveals a complex interplay of conformity and the innate human desire to belong. Conformity, a cornerstone of social psychology, is an essential component of social proof, illustrating how individuals often align their beliefs and behaviors with those of a group, particularly in situations where the correct course of action is ambiguous. This phenomenon is vividly encapsulated in the groundbreaking conformity experiments conducted by Solomon Asch in the 1950s.

Asch's experiments involved a simple yet profoundly revealing task. Participants were shown a series of lines and asked to identify which line matched a reference line in length. What made the study fascinating was the presence of confederates – individuals who were in on the experiment and intentionally provided the wrong answers. The goal was to observe whether the lone participant would conform to the group's incorrect consensus or stick to their own judgment. The results were striking; a significant number of participants conformed to the incorrect answer at least once, demonstrating the powerful influence of group dynamics on individual choices.

Asch's work illuminated the fragile nature of human perception and judgment when placed under social pressure. It showed that the need for social acceptance and validation could drive individuals to contradict their own beliefs, as the desire to fit in often outweighs the need for accuracy. This psychological need for belonging extends beyond the confines of a laboratory experiment; it permeates our daily lives and shapes our choices, convincing us that aligning with the majority is not just safer, but often the preferred path.

The historical context of social proof further underscores its profound impact on human behavior. Throughout history, there have been numerous instances where the principles of social proof have been exploited to gain control over populations, often with devastating consequences. Totalitarian regimes, for example, have adeptly leveraged social proof to enforce conformity and suppress dissent, creating an environment in which individuals feel compelled to align with the dominant ideology.

Consider the chilling case of Nazi Germany, where the regime implemented orchestrated propaganda campaigns, creating a facade of unanimous support for its policies. The Nazi Party's ability to showcase large rallies filled with fervent supporters was a strategic move to create an illusion of social proof, persuading ordinary citizens that backing the regime was not only the norm but a necessity. Such tactics instilled fear in dissenters and reinforced conformity among the populace, demonstrating the dark side of social proof when wielded by those in power.

There are also countless moments in history where social proof has catalyzed significant societal change. The civil rights movement in the United States, for instance, was marked by collective action that capitalized on the idea of social proof. Public demonstrations, including the famous March on Washington, drew immense crowds, signaling widespread support for racial equality. The visibility of thousands coming together for a common cause inspired others to join the movement, creating a ripple effect that eventually led to substantial changes in legislation and societal attitudes toward race.

The psychological mechanisms of social proof are deeply woven into the fabric of our social interactions. People tend to look for cues from others when navigating unfamiliar situations, and this instinctual behavior often shapes their actions more than they realize. As we progress into contemporary society, it becomes essential to recognize the implications of social proof in the digital age, where social media platforms amplify its effects exponentially.

In our interconnected world, the dynamics of social proof have evolved, presenting new challenges and opportunities for understanding human behavior. The massive sway of online communities and influencers showcases how social proof continues to play a pivotal role in shaping preferences, from product endorsements to political opinions. By analyzing these contemporary applications, we can gain valuable insights into the persistent and profound influence of social proof in our lives.

In summary, social proof serves as a powerful psychological mechanism that guides our decision-making processes in ways both subtle and overt. Through examining historical contexts, psychological theories, and contemporary applications, we gain a deeper understanding of why humans are inclined to follow the crowd, often at the expense of individuality. As we now move forward, it is time to explore the myriad ways in which social proof manifests in modern society, illuminating its significance in shaping our choices and behaviors in an increasingly interconnected world.

In the ever-evolving landscape of contemporary marketing and social media, the phenomenon of social proof has become a cornerstone for driving consumer behavior and shaping societal trends. To look deeply into this subject, one must first understand what social proof entails. It is the psychological phenomenon where individuals look to the behaviors and opinions of others to guide their own actions, particularly in situations of uncertainty. The power of social proof is particularly prominent in today's world, where the impact of digital communication and global connectivity has amplified its reach.

Influencer marketing, a prominent strategy within the realm of social proof, exemplifies how brands harness the sway of individuals who have amassed significant followings on social media platforms. These influencers, from beauty gurus to lifestyle coaches, cultivate a perceived authenticity that resonates with their audience. When they showcase a product or endorse a brand, their followers are often compelled to imitate their choices, believing that the influencers' suggestions are genuine reflections of quality and desirability. This phenomenon is further intensified by the viral nature of social media, where trends can spread like wildfire, fueled by likes, shares, and retweets. A prime example of this is the Ice Bucket Challenge, which swept across platforms like Facebook and Twitter in 2014.

The Ice Bucket Challenge was not only a viral sensation but also a powerful demonstration of social proof in action. Individuals across the globe poured buckets of icy water over themselves to raise awareness for amyotrophic lateral sclerosis (ALS) and subsequently challenged their friends to do the same. The challenge's success was bolstered by the endorsement of celebrities and influencers who participated, showcasing a classic case of how social proof can mobilize large groups toward a common cause.

However, the impact of social proof extends beyond altruistic movements. It profoundly influences consumer behavior in ways that can be both beneficial and detrimental. Online reviews serve as another significant manifestation of social proof, where potential buyers are swayed by the experiences and opinions of prior customers. For instance, platforms like Yelp and TripAdvisor have transformed the decision-making process for restaurants, hotels, and experiences, often elevating businesses that accumulate positive reviews while simultaneously endangering those that fail to meet expectations.

Businesses increasingly leverage these dynamics of social proof to manipulate consumer choices. For example, showcasing a high volume of positive user-generated content can create an illusion of widespread approval. This tactic isn't merely about presenting favorable reviews; it's about curating a narrative that positions the product or service as a societal norm. When consumers see that many others have made a purchase or endorsed a brand, they may feel compelled to conform to that behavior, often without a thorough evaluation of their own needs or the merits of the product itself.

As we navigate this landscape marked by pervasive social proof, it becomes imperative for individuals to recognize and resist the conformity pressures that seek to dictate their choices. To do so effectively, one must cultivate a set of practical tools and strategies to identify when they are being influenced by social proof. Critical thinking skills emerge as essential allies in this endeavor. By questioning the motives behind marketing strategies or the authenticity of endorsements, individuals can distance themselves from the subtle coercion of the crowd.

It is crucial to develop a questioning mindset that encourages individuals to seek diverse perspectives rather than simply accepting the status quo. For instance, instead of relying solely on aggregated online ratings, consumers might benefit from exploring product specifications, expert reviews, and alternative viewpoints. This approach not only fosters a more nuanced understanding of choices but also empowers individuals to make decisions that genuinely align with their values and needs.

In the face of societal pressures, fostering individual agency and self-awareness in decision-making processes is paramount. Recognizing that every purchasing decision or social action reflects personal values can help reinforce one's autonomy and discernment. When faced with a trend or a popular recommendation, asking oneself, "Does this align with my principles?" can serve as a vital checkpoint.

Moreover, the value of independent thought cannot be overstated. In a culture that often celebrates consensus and conformity, cultivating a questioning mindset becomes an act of bravery. The potential consequences of unchecked conformity extend far beyond personal choices; they can significantly impact democratic processes and social accountability.

When individuals opt to prioritize collective acceptance over personal conviction, the risks are manifold. For instance, in democratic societies, the failure to question prevailing norms can lead to the erosion of individual rights and liberties. The herd mentality can stifle dissenting voices, allowing authoritarian ideologies to flourish unchallenged. Additionally, social accountability diminishes when people prioritize conformity over integrity.

Thus, the call to action for readers is one of vigilance—an appeal to remain alert against the subtle influences of crowd mentality. Social proof can be a powerful motivator, yet understanding its mechanisms equips individuals with the tools needed to navigate its effects critically. By maintaining a mindset of inquiry and encouraging discourse that welcomes diverse opinions, we can foster a culture that values independent thought over blind conformity.

In conclusion, recognizing the significance of social proof in the context of propaganda and modern marketing is imperative for anyone seeking to navigate the complexities of today's social landscape. The influence of social proof is palpable, pervading our purchasing decisions, social interactions, and even our beliefs. Yet, by empowering ourselves with critical thinking skills and fostering independent thought, we can resist the pervasive pull of conformity and make choices that truly reflect our values.

As we continue to explore the intricate dynamics between social influence and individual agency, let us remain steadfast in our commitment to question, to challenge, and to engage with the world around us in a way that honors our unique perspectives. The journey toward self-awareness is not only personal; it is a collective endeavor that shapes the very fabric of our society.

In the aftermath of World War II, a haunting phrase echoed through the corridors of power and public discourse alike: "The bigger the lie, the more people will believe it." This notion can be traced back to the propaganda strategies employed by Adolf Hitler and his regime, which artfully manipulated the truth to galvanize an entire nation. Hitler understood that by perpetuating grandiose falsehoods with audacity, he could shape public sentiment and create a narrative so compelling that it would drown out dissenting voices. In contemporary society, we find echoes of this tactic in modern misinformation campaigns that proliferate across social media platforms, where sensationalist headlines and fabricated news stories can gain traction faster than ever.

The significance of the Big Lie extends far beyond mere deception; it is a powerful psychological tool that can reconfigure reality itself, influencing everything from political landscapes to social norms. The Big Lie technique plays a crucial role in molding public perception, and understanding its impact is essential in a world where misinformation can significantly alter the trajectory of societies. As we look deeper into this phenomenon, let us first examine its core concepts and how they operate within the human psyche.

At its core, the Big Lie is defined by two principal elements: audacity and repetition. The audacity of the statement—its sheer enormity—creates a cognitive dissonance that some individuals find difficult to reconcile. When faced with an assertion so grandiose, people may dismiss their inner skepticism out of hand, simply because the claim seems too outrageous to be false. This is compounded by the principle of repetition; the more a lie is told, the more it becomes entrenched in the collective consciousness.

Cognitive biases play a pivotal role in the effectiveness of the Big Lie. One such bias is confirmation bias, wherein individuals are predisposed to favor information that aligns with their pre-existing beliefs while neglecting or dismissing information that contradicts those beliefs. This bias creates fertile ground for the Big Lie to take root, as people unconsciously seek out narratives that reinforce their worldview.

Alongside confirmation bias, we encounter the illusory truth effect, a psychological phenomenon that illustrates how repeated exposure to false information can lead individuals to accept it as truth. Even when confronted with clear evidence to the contrary, the mere familiarity of the lie can create an illusion of truth. This effect is particularly insidious in today's information-rich environment, where the sheer volume of content can overwhelm our cognitive faculties, making it easier for falsehoods to slip through the cracks of our scrutiny.

Psychological research supports the effectiveness of the Big Lie technique, highlighting how these biases interact to create a powerful feedback loop of deception. For instance, studies have shown that when participants are repeatedly exposed to false statements, they are more likely to rate those statements as true, even after being informed of their inaccuracy. This raises alarming questions about the vulnerability of our collective consciousness to manipulation.

Real-world implications of the Big Lie can be observed in various domains, particularly in politics and media. In the realm of politics, we have witnessed the rise of populist leaders who have skillfully wielded the Big Lie to galvanize their bases. Consider the 2016 U.S. presidential election, during which a barrage of misinformation flooded social media platforms. False claims about voter fraud and other fabricated narratives circulated widely, contributing to a political climate marked by division and distrust.

In media, the Big Lie has found a willing partner in sensationalism, where news outlets sometimes prioritize clicks over accuracy. The proliferation of "fake news" has created an environment where individuals often struggle to discern fact from fiction. This symbiotic relationship between the Big Lie and media sensationalism further complicates our understanding of truth in an age characterized by rapid information dissemination.

To illustrate the potency of the Big Lie, we can examine specific case studies from history that demonstrate its application. One notable example is the disinformation campaign surrounding the Gulf of Tonkin incident during the Vietnam War. The U.S. government claimed that North Vietnamese forces had attacked American naval vessels, a narrative used to justify escalating military involvement in Vietnam.

However, subsequent investigations revealed that the events had been exaggerated or even fabricated. This deliberate manipulation of information had profound consequences, resulting in a protracted conflict that left lasting scars on both American soldiers and Vietnamese civilians. The Gulf of Tonkin incident serves as a poignant reminder of how the Big Lie can distort reality and lead to tragic outcomes.

Another powerful case study can be found in the realm of social movements. The Black Lives Matter movement, born from the outcry against systemic racism and police brutality, has faced its own share of misinformation campaigns. Detractors have employed the Big Lie technique to paint the movement as violent or extremist, seeking to undermine its legitimacy.

Despite these efforts, many individuals have resisted these narratives, driven by personal experiences and a commitment to social justice. Their stories reveal the resilience of truth and the power of collective action in the face of deception. These anecdotes highlight the importance of recognizing and challenging the Big Lie, as well as the necessity of engaging with facts and evidence in a world increasingly inundated with falsehoods.

The broader implications of the Big Lie for democracy and public discourse cannot be overstated. When truth is distorted and manipulated, the very foundation of democratic society is undermined. A healthy democracy relies on informed citizens who can engage in reasoned debate and hold their leaders accountable. The Big Lie erodes trust in institutions and complicates efforts to engage in meaningful dialogue, ultimately leading to polarization and division.

As we navigate this complex landscape, it is imperative for readers to cultivate critical thinking skills and a healthy skepticism toward the information they encounter. Engaging with diverse perspectives, questioning narratives, and seeking out reliable sources can empower individuals to resist the allure of the Big Lie.

In an age where misinformation is rampant, the ability to discern truth from falsehood is more crucial than ever. The Big Lie technique serves as a stark reminder of the power of words and the profound impact they can have on our beliefs, behaviors, and societal structures. By understanding the mechanisms behind the Big Lie, we can better equip ourselves to navigate the treacherous waters of modern discourse, fostering a more informed and resilient society.

The journey toward truth in a world rife with deception may be fraught with challenges, but it is a pursuit worth undertaking. Only by confronting the Big Lie head-on can we hope to foster a culture of honesty, integrity, and accountability that is essential for the health of our democracy and the well-being of our communities. As we forge ahead, let us remain vigilant, recognizing that the truth is not merely a passive state of being, but an active pursuit—one that requires courage, critical thinking, and an unwavering commitment to seek out the facts, even in the face of a world that often seems determined to obscure them.

Chapter 7: Psychological Manipulations

The intricate web of human thought and behavior is often woven with threads of fascinating psychological principles that, while deeply rooted in the fabric of our consciousness, operate subtly, almost invisibly. Among these principles is classical conditioning, a concept that not only helps us understand how learning occurs but also provides insight into the ways in which propaganda can exploit our psychological predispositions. This chapter aims to explore the nuances of classical conditioning, particularly its application in the realm of propaganda, where it serves as a formidable tool for shaping thoughts, beliefs, and behaviors.

The foundation of our understanding of classical conditioning is built upon the pioneering work of Ivan Pavlov, a Russian physiologist whose experiments with dogs in the late 19th century unveiled the astonishing mechanisms of associative learning. In his now-famous experiment, Pavlov observed that dogs would salivate not only in response to food but also when they heard the sound of a bell that had previously been paired with the presentation of food. This phenomenon, which he termed "classical conditioning," illustrates how a neutral stimulus (the bell) can acquire the ability to elicit a response (salivation) through repeated association with an unconditioned stimulus (food).

Pavlov's findings have profound implications beyond the confines of a laboratory. The principles of classical conditioning extend into the realm of propaganda, where the objective is often to create strong associations between particular ideas, images, or narratives and emotional responses. In the context of propaganda, a message that might initially seem neutral can be imbued with significant emotional weight through strategic pairing with positively or negatively charged stimuli. This transition from the "big lie," an explicit distortion of truth, to the subtler manipulation of perceptions through classical conditioning underscores the need for a deeper understanding of how our minds can be conditioned to accept information uncritically.

At its core, classical conditioning is a form of associative learning that allows individuals to make connections between seemingly unrelated stimuli. In the context of propaganda, this means that an organization or political entity can craft messages that resonate on an emotional level by linking them with symbols, imagery, or narratives that evoke strong feelings. For instance, consider a political advertisement that features a charismatic leader paired with patriotic music and images of a flourishing nation. The emotional response elicited by the visuals and sounds can create a powerful association in the viewer's mind, whereby the leader becomes synonymous with the feelings of pride, hope, and community.

This emotional pairing is not mere happenstance; it is a deliberate strategy employed by propagandists to embed their messages within the psyche of their audience. The aim is to ensure that when individuals encounter the leader or the political message later, the positive feelings previously associated with them are automatically activated. This is how propaganda thrives—by embedding itself within the emotional landscape of those it seeks to influence.

Let us look into the real-world applications of classical conditioning in advertising and political messaging, where its effects can be both pervasive and profound. Take, for example, the iconic advertising campaigns that have shaped consumer culture. Companies often utilize classical conditioning to create brand loyalty. A popular soft drink brand may consistently feature fun, joyous scenes of people enjoying their product at summer parties, accompanied by upbeat music and energetic visuals. Over time, consumers begin to associate the brand not just with refreshment, but with happiness, camaraderie, and celebration. Thus, when faced with the choice of a beverage, consumers are more likely to gravitate towards that brand because it has become ingrained in their emotional memory.

Political organizations and movements have adeptly harnessed this principle as well. Consider a campaign that repeatedly uses imagery of national monuments, flags, or historical figures who evoke strong patriotic sentiments. The continuous pairing of these symbols with the candidate's image or policies creates an automatic emotional response that aligns the candidate with national pride and identity. Audiences may not consciously recognize this manipulation; instead, they feel an instinctive sense of allegiance or trust towards the candidate, rooted in the emotional resonance of the imagery they have absorbed over time.

Case studies abound that illustrate this dynamic at play. During wartime, governments have often utilized propaganda to bolster public support for military actions. The use of evocative imagery—perhaps depicting heroic soldiers, grieving families, or triumphant victories—coupled with stirring narratives creates a rich tapestry of emotional associations. When citizens repeatedly encounter this blend of visuals and stories in the media, they become conditioned to react favorably to the idea of war, seeing it not merely as a conflict but as a noble endeavor.

One particularly striking example can be found in the propaganda campaigns employed during World War II.

Governments on both sides sought to instill a sense of duty and urgency among their citizens. Posters depicting brave soldiers, heart-wrenching images of families waiting for their loved ones, and stirring slogans like "Support Our Troops!" played on deep emotional currents. The repeated exposure to these messages conditioned the public to respond with fervent patriotism, often blurring the lines between informed consent and blind allegiance.

However, the effects of classical conditioning are not confined to advertising and political propaganda. They extend into the personal experiences of individuals and communities, often weaving through their narratives in unexpected ways. Consider the story of an individual who remembers their childhood experiences with a particular brand of cereal. Each morning, the bright, colorful box adorned with cartoon characters was accompanied by the warmth of family togetherness and laughter around the breakfast table. Decades later, when confronted with a similar product in a grocery store, an involuntary rush of nostalgia and happiness could flood their consciousness, leading them to purchase the cereal out of sheer emotional association rather than a rational evaluation of its nutritional value.

This phenomenon illustrates the capacity for classical conditioning to shape not only consumer habits but also our understanding of ourselves and our identities. The stories we tell ourselves about our preferences and choices are often grounded in the emotional experiences we have associated with various stimuli over time. As such, individuals may find themselves drawn towards certain ideologies, products, or even relationships based largely on the conditioning they have undergone throughout their lives.

Yet, amid this pervasive influence, there lies the potential for resistance and awareness. While classical conditioning operates subtly, individuals possess the ability to recognize and question the associations being made on their behalf. It is not uncommon for individuals to become conscious of the manipulative tactics employed by advertisers and propagandists, leading to a degree of skepticism toward the messages they encounter.

The capacity for resistance, however, hinges on education and critical thinking. By fostering an awareness of classical conditioning, individuals can become more attuned to the emotional triggers embedded within the narratives they consume, prompting them to question their validity and motives. This awareness empowers citizens to sift through the noise of propaganda and discern the motivations behind the messages being presented to them.

In recent years, there has been a growing discourse around media literacy, emphasizing the importance of teaching individuals, particularly young people, to navigate the complex landscape of information. By equipping individuals with the skills to critically engage with the media they consume, society can cultivate a generation that is not only aware of the manipulative techniques employed within propaganda but also capable of resisting them.

As we reflect on the importance of recognizing classical conditioning in our daily lives, it is clear that the implications extend far beyond the realm of advertising or political messaging. They permeate our social interactions, relationships, and identity formation. The ability to identify and analyze the narrative techniques that shape our experiences enhances our capacity for informed citizenship, enabling us to engage critically with the world around us.

In conclusion, classical conditioning serves as a powerful lens through which to examine the mechanisms of psychological manipulation inherent in propaganda. The associations we form through repeated exposure to emotionally charged stimuli can profoundly influence our beliefs, behaviors, and perceptions. By cultivating awareness of these dynamics, we empower ourselves to navigate the complexities of modern life with a critical eye, ensuring that we remain vigilant against the subtle manipulations that seek to shape our understanding of reality.

Ultimately, the goal of this exploration is to foster informed citizenship and a commitment to critical engagement with the narratives that permeate our lives. As we strive to cultivate an environment where individuals can question and analyze the messages they encounter, we lay the groundwork for a more enlightened society—one in which the power of classical conditioning is recognized and understood, rather than blindly accepted. Thus, by embracing our capacity for reflection and analysis, we can forge a path toward a more thoughtful and discerning engagement with the world around us.

Chapter 8: The Power of Presentation

In today's world, information flows at lightning speed, and the way that information is presented can drastically alter its reception and interpretation. To illustrate the profound impact that framing can have on public perception, we can reflect on the events surrounding a notable political rally that took place just a few years ago. Imagine a gathering, charged with energy, where supporters gathered beneath banners and placards, each vying for attention in a sea of slogans and rhetoric. Some supporters spoke passionately about "freedom" and "empowerment," while others voiced concerns about "oppression" and "injustice."

At the same event, however, the media's portrayal ran the gamut from celebratory coverage underscoring the enthusiasm of activists to critical reports focusing on isolated incidents of unruly behavior. This divergence in presentation highlights a critical element of communication: framing. Framing refers to the process of emphasizing certain aspects of information while downplaying or omitting others. It is not merely about what is said but how it is said, effectively shaping the narrative and guiding public perception in specific directions. The event's framing—whether framed as a triumph of democratic expression or a chaotic disturbance—had the power to influence not only the opinions of those who attended but also those who followed the news from afar.

Understanding framing requires us to look deeper into its psychological underpinnings. Our brains are wired to seek patterns and make sense of information, but this can lead us to develop cognitive biases—systematic deviations from rationality in judgment. For example, consider confirmation bias, where individuals favor information that aligns with their existing beliefs while disregarding contradicting evidence. When we encounter framed information, our cognitive processes can unwittingly reinforce these biases. The way information is framed can trigger specific association pathways in our brains, leading to certain interpretations while obscuring others.

Moreover, the way we process framed information is influenced by our emotional state and previous experiences. When a political figure is described as a "revolutionary" versus a "radical," the emotional weight of those terms can elicit vastly different responses. Not only do these terms connote varied connotations, they also tap into existing beliefs and feelings, thus affecting how individuals perceive the person being described. Our susceptibility to these framing tactics can be attributed to both our cognitive architecture and the emotional resonance of particular words or phrases.

This leads us to the concept of loaded language, a powerful tool in shaping opinions and influencing public discourse. Loaded language is characterized by words or phrases that carry strong emotional implications, appealing to an audience's feelings rather than their rationality. The significance of loaded language lies in its ability to conjure vivid images, stir emotions, and polarize opinions. Consider the terms "pro-life" and "anti-abortion." The former suggests a stance that values life, while the latter implies opposition to a choice that many view as a personal right. The choice of language here is not trivial; these terms encapsulate entire ideologies and evoke strong emotional responses, thus framing the debate around abortion in a way that reflects the speaker's values.

Neutral language, in contrast, seeks to describe situations or opinions without emotional weight. A phrase like "individual choice regarding reproductive health" lacks the same charged connotations and, as a result, can foster a more balanced discussion. However, the prevalence of loaded language in media, politics, and everyday discourse makes it challenging for audiences to engage critically with issues. Emotional responses can easily overshadow rational examination, pushing individuals to adopt positions based on feelings rather than facts.

To understand the ramifications of framing and loaded language in practice, we can examine a case study involving a recent media campaign that effectively leveraged these techniques to sway public opinion. The campaign in question revolved around environmental regulations aimed at reducing carbon emissions. Advocates for the regulations framed their messaging around the concept of "clean air for our children," evoking images of a healthier future and societal responsibility. This framing appealed to parents' instincts to protect their children and fostered a sense of urgency and moral obligation.

In stark contrast, opponents of the regulations deployed a different framing strategy, describing the policies as "job-killing regulations" that would lead to economic collapse. This framing sought to elicit fear and anxiety regarding potential job losses and economic instability, effectively swaying public sentiment towards opposition. As the campaign unfolded, media outlets played their role in amplifying these competing narratives, leading to a fractured public discourse about environmental responsibility versus economic stability.

By dissecting the messaging methods used in this campaign, we can observe how specific framing elements influenced public perception. The phrase "clean air for our children" not only evokes a sense of hope and responsibility but also paints a stark contrast to the dystopian vision presented by the opposition. As a result, those exposed to these competing messages may find themselves swayed by the emotional resonance of one framing over another, leading to polarized opinions on an issue that demands nuanced discussion.

The implications of framing extend beyond individual opinions; they ripple through societal attitudes and democratic discourse. When public conversations are dominated by emotionally charged language and simplified narratives, the risk of miscommunication and misunderstanding escalates. As citizens become entrenched in their viewpoints, it becomes increasingly difficult to engage in constructive dialogue that could bridge divides and lead to collaborative solutions. The art of framing, therefore, is not simply a manipulation of words; it represents a profound influence on the collective consciousness.

In conclusion, understanding the mechanisms of framing and the power of loaded language is crucial for anyone navigating the complex terrain of public discourse. As we continue to unpack these concepts, we must remain vigilant about how information is presented and the emotional weight of the words we encounter. By sharpening our critical thinking skills and questioning the framing of narratives, we can foster a more informed and engaged society, capable of addressing the pressing challenges that lie ahead. Empowering ourselves with this knowledge not only enhances our personal comprehension but also reinforces the foundation of democratic discourse, enabling a richer and more nuanced exchange of ideas.

In today's fast-paced digital world, the language we encounter daily influences our perceptions, shapes our beliefs, and subsequently guides our actions. Language is not merely a tool for communication; it is a powerful instrument that can shape narratives, evoke emotions, and ultimately manipulate the way we think. We will look into the critical task of identifying and challenging biased language in media, equipping readers with practical strategies to recognize euphemisms, emotionally charged language, and biased terminology.

We will explore how to engage with media critically, develop a heightened awareness of language manipulation, and understand the implications of our findings on democratic dialogue.

The first step towards countering biased language is recognizing it when we encounter it. Euphemisms—those seemingly benign phrases that soften harsh realities—are often a red flag for bias. For instance, consider the term "collateral damage." While this phrase might be used to describe the unintended consequences of military actions, it obfuscates the fact that this "damage" frequently includes the loss of innocent lives. Recognizing such language requires a discerning eye: we must ask ourselves what is being concealed behind the veil of euphemism.

Emotionally charged language, too, serves as a mechanism for bias. Words loaded with emotional weight can elicit strong reactions, shaping public sentiment and opinion. For example, a news article might refer to a group of protestors as "an angry mob," invoking images of chaos and violence, while a similar group advocating for change may be described as "passionate activists." As readers, we must interrogate the language employed in the narratives we consume, questioning who benefits from the emotional framing of the situation.

In addition to euphemisms and emotionally charged language, biased terminology can often pervade media discussions. Labels such as "radical" or "extremist" can delegitimize individuals or groups, encouraging a dismissive attitude without engaging with their ideas. To challenge biased terminology, we encourage readers to cultivate a habit of actively engaging with current media examples for real-time analysis. Whether it's a news segment, an editorial, or even a social media post, take a moment to dissect the language used. What terms stand out? How might the choice of words influence the perception of the subject at hand?

To further hone our skills in recognizing biased language, let us adopt a step-by-step approach to dissecting news articles and political speeches. Start with the headline; it often sets the tone for the entire piece. Analyze it critically: is it sensationalized? Does it invoke a particular emotion? Next, read through the content with a focus on the descriptors. Notice how people, events, and issues are framed. Are there underlying assumptions that skew the narrative?

Throughout this analysis, it is paramount to question the narrative itself. Whose voice is being amplified? Whose is being silenced? Are there alternative perspectives that challenge the dominant storyline? Engaging with diverse sources can be illuminating. For instance, when examining a political speech, seek out transcripts or analyses from multiple outlets. What language choices do they emphasize? By contrasting different portrayals, you can gain insight into the biases that permeate various narratives.

Moreover, it's important to foster a critical mindset not just in our media consumption, but in our everyday conversations about contentious issues. This requires us to be vigilant about our own language as well. How do we frame our arguments? Are we perpetuating biases unintentionally? By being aware of our language, we can foster more constructive dialogues that welcome diverse perspectives and promote understanding rather than division.

The journey towards empowerment through awareness begins with recognizing how pervasive language manipulation is in our daily lives. Every time we engage with news media, read social media posts, or even participate in casual dialogue, we are confronted with the potential for language to distort reality. By cultivating an awareness of this dynamic, we equip ourselves to navigate the complexities of communication more effectively.

Ultimately, the role of an informed citizenry in promoting healthy democratic dialogue cannot be overstated. Citizens who are cognizant of the language used in media and politics can challenge narratives that seek to divide or manipulate. When we approach discussions with a critical lens, we foster an environment where healthy debate can thrive, encouraging understanding and collaboration among diverse groups.

As we conclude our exploration of biased language, it is essential to revisit the key concepts of framing and language manipulation. Recognizing euphemisms, emotionally charged language, and biased terminology is just the beginning. The real challenge lies in our commitment to engage critically with the narratives we encounter, to question the assumptions and motivations behind the language choices made by those in power.

In doing so, we not only enhance our understanding of the world around us; we also contribute to a culture of critical engagement that promotes dialogue over division. As we navigate the complexities of communication in an increasingly polarized society, let us embrace the challenge of fostering a critical mindset—both in our media interactions and in our everyday discussions about contentious issues.

In conclusion, the importance of recognizing and challenging biased language cannot be overstated. It is incumbent upon each of us to take the reins of our understanding and navigate the nuanced landscape of language in media. Through active engagement and a commitment to questioning narratives, we become part of a larger movement towards informed discourse, where healthy dialogue prevails over misinformation and manipulation. Let us move forward with a renewed sense of purpose, armed with the knowledge that our words matter, and so does our ability to wield them with intention and integrity.

Chapter 9: Charismatic Manipulation

In the sepulchral glow of late afternoon, the vast expanse of a stadium pulsated with energy, the kind that ripples through a crowd like an electric current. Amidst this sea of humanity, faces radiated anticipation, excitement, and a hint of desperation, as if they were collectively holding their breath waiting for something transformative to sweep through their ranks. The air was thick with chants, slogans that echoed like mantras—words that had been repeated so often they had morphed into an almost hypnotic spell. On the stage, a figure emerged, silhouetted against a backdrop of fervent supporters, clad in a tailored suit that spoke of authority and confidence. This was not just a leader; this was a prophet, a savior in the eyes of many.

The moment the leader raised their hand to address the crowd, the atmosphere shifted palpably. The sound of clapping surged like a tidal wave, drowning out any dissenting thoughts. As the speaker began to talk, their voice oscillated between calm authority and fervent passion, each word carefully crafted to resonate with the deep-seated hopes and collective anxieties of those gathered. The charisma radiating from this individual was palpable—infusing the crowd with a sense of purpose, unity, and belonging that was intoxicating. As the speech unfolded, it became increasingly evident that this was not merely a political gathering; it was the very embodiment of what has come to be known as the "cult of personality."

The term "cult of personality" refers to the phenomenon wherein a public figure—often a political leader—gains a substantial following largely due to their personal charisma rather than their policies or ideologies. It signifies the elevation of an individual to a near-mythical status, where their image becomes synonymous with the identity of a movement or cause. This dynamic is profound, for it highlights a fundamental aspect of human psychology: the tendency to idolize figures who evoke strong emotions, inspire loyalty, and create a sense of belonging. In essence, the cult of personality underscores a critical intersection between psychology and propaganda, revealing how deeply our individual and collective psyches are influenced by charismatic figures.

At the core of charismatic manipulation lies a series of psychological mechanisms that work in concert to foster an unshakeable bond between the leader and their followers. One of the most powerful of these mechanisms is identification. When individuals feel an intense connection with a charismatic leader, they often begin to see parts of themselves reflected in that leader's persona. This process is not merely superficial; it runs deep within the human psyche. Followers may adopt the leader's beliefs, language, and mannerisms, creating a sense of shared identity.

Emotional contagion further amplifies this identification. In a group setting, emotions can spread like wildfire. When a leader expresses passion, confidence, or even anger, those emotions can be unconsciously absorbed by the crowd. This phenomenon is particularly pronounced in political rallies, where followers are not just passive spectators but active participants in a collective emotional experience. The laughter, the tears, the shouts of agreement—all of these responses become intertwined in a powerful tapestry of emotion that can lead to heightened loyalty and fervor.

Equally significant is the universal human need for belonging. Psychologists have long emphasized that humans are inherently social creatures, driven by a psychological imperative to connect with others. Charismatic leaders exploit this need masterfully. They create an environment where followers feel seen, heard, and valued. The leader's rhetoric often emphasizes a shared struggle, a common enemy, or a unifying cause, all of which serve to strengthen the in-group bond. By positioning themselves as the embodiment of these ideals, leaders can effectively manipulate their followers' emotions, fostering unwavering loyalty and commitment.

The role of charisma itself is a fascinating topic within the realm of psychology. Defined as a compelling charm or appeal, charisma operates on several levels, influencing perception and behavior. Carismatic individuals often exude confidence, warmth, and decisiveness, which can create a magnetic pull towards them. This contagion is not merely about the person; it's about the energy they generate. In a charismatic leader, followers often perceive an aura of certainty and power that offers them reassurance in uncertain times. The leader becomes a focal point for their hopes and aspirations, a figure who promises salvation or redemption.

Historically, the power of charismatic manipulation has been evident through various leaders who have shaped the course of nations and societies. Adolf Hitler stands as a stark testament to the effective use of charisma intertwined with psychological manipulation. His speeches were not merely political assertions but grand performances that stirred the souls of those who listened. With his unique oratory skills, he could evoke a range of emotions—from fervent patriotism to visceral anger—leading his followers to see their own struggles reflected in his narrative. The psychological impact of his rhetoric was profound, inciting a fervor that propelled a nation into darkness.

Contrastingly, the charismatic appeal of John F. Kennedy illustrated a different facet of manipulation. Kennedy's charm was a blend of warmth, relatability, and intellectual rigor. His ability to connect with the American public was palpable, as he often framed complex issues in ways that were accessible and inspiring. His famous inaugural address, with its call to civic duty and collective responsibility, encapsulated his ability to galvanize a nation towards a shared vision of progress. Kennedy's charisma was not merely about personal magnetism; it was about mobilizing a populace through a narrative that emphasized hope and potential.

Examining these leaders reveals common elements that characterize charismatic manipulation across different contexts. The ability to articulate a vision—one that resonates with the deep-seated desires and fears of followers—is paramount. Furthermore, the savvy use of emotional appeals—whether through stirring oratory, visual symbols, or group dynamics—creates an environment ripe for manipulation. Charismatic leaders also exhibit a remarkable skill in understanding and tapping into the zeitgeist of their time; they become the conduits through which collective anxieties and hopes are channeled.

In conclusion, the psychological foundations of charismatic manipulation reveal a complex interplay of identification, emotional contagion, and the intrinsic human need for belonging. Charismatic leaders wield significant power, not just because of their position, but because they forge deep emotional connections with their followers. Through history, these connections have been instrumental in shaping movements and ideologies, demonstrating the profound impact charisma can have on collective human behavior. As we look deeper into the mechanics of charismatic manipulation, it becomes essential to recognize both its potential for positive influence and its capacity to lead societies astray. Understanding these dynamics not only informs our grasp of history but also equips us to navigate the turbulent waters of contemporary leadership and influence.

In the landscape of the 21st century, the potency of charismatic manipulation has evolved into a phenomenon that pervades our daily lives, transforming the way we consume information, interact with each other, and navigate the complexities of societal discourse. As social media platforms burgeon, figures of influence emerge not only as authorities in their respective domains but also as catalysts for both connection and division. This chapter looks into the intricate dynamics of contemporary charismatic manipulation, focusing particularly on the rise of social media influencers, the implications of their sway, and ultimately, the necessity for critical thinking in an increasingly polarized world.

The emergence of social media influencers represents a seismic shift in the way charisma and influence are defined and exercised. Platforms like Instagram and TikTok have birthed a new generation of charismatic personalities who wield their charm and relatability in ways that traditional media figures simply cannot match. Unlike the past, where authority often resided in the hands of journalists, academics, or political leaders, today's influencers cultivate their followings by presenting themselves as accessible, relatable, and authentic. The curated glimpses into their lives, often embellished for effect, create a bond of connection that feels genuine to their audience. It's an illusion of intimacy that fosters trust and admiration, which are leveraged to propel their messages, whether they're advocating for a lifestyle, a product, or even a political ideology.

This phenomenon of influencer culture blurs the lines between influence and authority. In the digital landscape, the criteria for authority have shifted. No longer is expertise a prerequisite for being taken seriously; instead, followers often conflate popularity with credibility. A fitness influencer, for example, may gain a massive following for their aesthetic appeal and charismatic presentation of workouts, yet lack any formal training in health or exercise science. Their fans, however, may heed their advice without question, mistaking charisma for competence. This shift raises critical questions about the nature of authority in the modern era. What does it mean to be authoritative? How do we discern valid expertise in a cacophonous marketplace of ideas where every influencer claims to have the answers?

The implications of charismatic manipulation extend far beyond individual interactions; they seep into the fabric of public discourse and democratic engagement. The rapid spread of misinformation has been exacerbated by charismatic figures who can craft compelling narratives that attract attention and engagement. Social media algorithms, designed to prioritize content that garners the most interactions, inadvertently amplify the voices of those who can stir emotion or controversy—often at the expense of truth. This poses a significant threat to democratic discourse, where informed debate is fundamental to the functioning of society. When a charismatic figure promotes a distorted version of reality, their followers may be swayed to adopt beliefs that not only lack foundation but also contribute to societal discord.

Moreover, the prevalence of emotional appeals over rational discourse represents another perilous trend in contemporary society. Charismatic manipulators often harness the power of emotion to rally support for their causes, using fear, anger, or joy as tools to galvanize their audiences. While emotional engagement is an integral part of human communication, the prioritization of feelings over facts can lead to deeply entrenched divisions. As individuals gravitate toward narratives that resonate with their emotions, they may overlook the need for critical analysis and rational dialogue. The danger lies in the potential for echo chambers to form, where dissenting views are silenced, and the discourse becomes increasingly polarized.

In the face of these challenges, fostering critical thinking emerges as an essential strategy for navigating an era rife with charismatic manipulation. Recognizing manipulation when it occurs is the first step toward empowering oneself as a consumer of information. It is crucial for individuals to approach charismatic figures with a discerning mindset, asking themselves probing questions: What are the motivations behind this person's message? Are they presenting a balanced perspective, or are they selectively amplifying certain narratives? By engaging in this self-reflective practice, individuals can begin to demystify the allure of charisma and make more informed decisions about the information they consume.

Encouraging skepticism is equally vital in fostering a culture of critical thinking. In a world where information is abundant yet often unreliable, questioning the validity of sources and claims becomes paramount. Skepticism, when properly applied, acts as a safeguard against manipulation. It invites individuals to seek out diverse viewpoints, engage with opposing arguments, and verify facts before forming conclusions. By cultivating this habit, individuals can break free from the constraints of charismatic manipulation and pave the way for a more informed and engaged citizenry.

Ultimately, the goal of this chapter is to empower readers with the awareness needed to recognize and analyze charismatic manipulation in its various forms. In doing so, we lay the groundwork for fostering informed citizenship and social responsibility. Awareness is a potent tool; through it, individuals can mitigate the risks associated with charismatic figures, ensuring that their engagement with information is grounded in critical thought rather than blind adherence to charm or popularity. We must strive to nurture an environment where rational discourse prevails, where emotional appeals are balanced by reasoned arguments, and where the lines between influence and authority are clearly defined.

In navigating the complexities of the modern era, we must remain vigilant stewards of our own minds. Charismatic manipulation, while a testament to the power of human connection, can also lead us astray if left unchecked. By cultivating critical thinking, encouraging skepticism, and recognizing the nuances of influence, we can empower ourselves and others to engage with information in a manner that fosters understanding, promotes dialogue, and ultimately strengthens the very foundations of our democratic society. The landscape of charismatic manipulation may be ever-evolving, but our commitment to informed engagement can serve as a bulwark against its more insidious tendencies, propelling us toward a future where charisma is wielded not for manipulation, but for inspiration, unity, and positive change.

They're Lying to You

Chapter 10: Discrediting The Opposition

In our contemporary society, the dissemination of information has reached an unprecedented scale, fueled by the rise of digital technology and social media platforms. As we navigate this vast ocean of information, we encounter a darker undercurrent: disinformation and smear campaigns, which have become potent tools wielded by those seeking to manipulate public opinion, shape political landscapes, and tarnish reputations. To effectively address these phenomena, it is crucial to first develop a comprehensive understanding of what disinformation and smear campaigns entail, how they function, and the psychological underpinnings that make them so effective.

Disinformation, at its core, refers to the intentional spread of false or misleading information with the specific goal of deceiving or manipulating individuals or groups. Unlike misinformation, which may simply involve the unintentional sharing of incorrect information, disinformation is strategically crafted and disseminated. The primary purpose of disinformation in the realm of propaganda is to sow confusion, create divisions, and undermine trust in legitimate sources of information. By orchestrating a well-timed and targeted campaign, disinformation can alter public perceptions, influence decision-making processes, and shift the overall narrative in favor of specific agendas.

Smear campaigns, on the other hand, represent a particular subset of disinformation that focuses on damaging the reputation of individuals—often political figures, activists, or organizations. These campaigns are designed to paint a negative image of the target, often through the use of distorted facts, exaggerated claims, or outright fabrications. Smear campaigns serve to discredit opponents, diminish their credibility, and ultimately deflect attention away from legitimate criticisms or discussions. By eroding public trust in a target, smear campaigns can effectively change the dynamics of competition, whether in politics, business, or social movements.

To fully appreciate the impact of disinformation and smear campaigns, we can examine several historical and contemporary examples that illustrate their machinations and effectiveness. One of the most illustrative cases in recent U.S. political history is the "Swift Boat Veterans for Truth" campaign against Senator John Kerry during the 2004 presidential election. This campaign was launched by a group of veterans who opposed Kerry's candidacy, asserting that he had misrepresented his service in the Vietnam War. The campaign leveraged a mix of half-truths, emotional appeals, and strategically timed advertisements to create doubt about Kerry's character and service record. Despite Kerry's commendable military service and his strong reputation among veterans, the smear campaign significantly altered public perception, leading to questions about his integrity and suitability for the presidency.

Similarly, the Brexit referendum in 2016 serves as a compelling example of the use of misinformation tactics to sway public opinion. During the campaign, both sides employed various strategies to disseminate information, but the Leave campaign, in particular, faced scrutiny for making bold claims that were demonstrably false. One notable example was the assertion that leaving the European Union would free up £350 million per week for the National Health Service (NHS), a figure that was later debunked. This misleading statistic painted a rosy picture of Brexit's potential benefits while obscuring the complexities and potential drawbacks of severing ties with the EU. The effectiveness of these misinformation tactics can be attributed to their emotional resonance, catching the attention of voters who were anxious about the future and eager for hopeful solutions.

As we look deeper into the psychological and social mechanisms that underpin the success of disinformation and smear campaigns, it becomes apparent that certain cognitive biases play a crucial role in their effectiveness. One significant bias is confirmation bias, which refers to the tendency of individuals to seek out and favor information that aligns with their preexisting beliefs while dismissing conflicting information. In an era saturated with information, individuals often gravitate towards narratives that reinforce their viewpoints, making them susceptible to disinformation that resonates with their biases. This means that once a person has been exposed to a smear campaign or disinformation that aligns with their beliefs, they are likely to accept it as truth and incorporate it into their worldview, further entrenching their biases.

Another relevant cognitive phenomenon is the illusory truth effect, which suggests that repeated exposure to a statement increases the likelihood of it being perceived as true, regardless of its actual validity. This effect underscores the power of repetition in disinformation campaigns, where the same false narratives are circulated across various platforms and formats, embedding them into the collective consciousness. As individuals encounter these repeated messages, they may become desensitized to the inaccuracies and ultimately accept them as factual. This dynamic creates a self-reinforcing cycle wherein misinformation becomes entrenched, complicating efforts to correct false narratives or counteract smear tactics.

Together, these psychological mechanisms create fertile ground for disinformation and smear campaigns to flourish. They exploit our natural cognitive tendencies, leveraging emotional appeals and repetition to manipulate perceptions and alter beliefs. To combat these efforts, it is essential for individuals and societies to cultivate critical thinking skills, promote media literacy, and foster an environment where discussions are grounded in evidence and rational discourse.

The implications of disinformation and smear campaigns extend beyond individual perceptions; they can shape societal narratives and influence political landscapes. As we grapple with the challenges posed by these phenomena, it becomes essential to engage with the complex interplay of technology, psychology, and communication that fuels their proliferation. By understanding how disinformation and smear campaigns operate, and the psychological mechanisms that contribute to their effectiveness, we can begin to develop strategies to counteract their impact and foster a more informed and engaged citizenry.

Chapter 10: The Impact of Disinformation and Tools for Resistance

In the present age, we find ourselves navigating an intricate labyrinth of information, where the line between truth and falsehood is increasingly blurred. Disinformation has spiraled into a pervasive force, altering our understanding of reality, undermining public trust in institutions, and threatening the very foundations of democratic processes. The consequences of misinformation are manifold, affecting public opinion, shaping policy changes, and deepening social divides. To combat this insidious phenomenon, it is essential to arm ourselves with a robust toolkit for discerning fact from fiction and engage actively with the media that surrounds us.

The erosion of trust in institutions is a silent yet significant consequence of the disinformation epidemic. Numerous studies have shed light on this alarming trend, revealing that trust in government, media, and scientific institutions has plummeted over the last few decades. The Edelman Trust Barometer, for instance, has shown a consistent decline in trust across the board, with a stark correlation between the rise of disinformation campaigns and the waning of public confidence. The data suggests that as people are bombarded with conflicting information, they become skeptical of almost everything, leading to a pervasive cynicism that can extend even to previously trusted sources.

Public opinion, an often volatile landscape, becomes further complicated when misinformation takes root. Take, for example, the issue of climate change. Campaigns aimed at sowing doubt about the scientific consensus have not only confused the public but have also influenced policy decisions. Legislators, swayed by the loud voices of misinformation, may hesitate to endorse policies aimed at addressing climate change due to perceived public dissent that is, in reality, a mirage crafted by manipulated information narratives. This dynamic creates a chilling effect, stymieing essential policy initiatives and prolonging societal challenges that could otherwise be addressed through informed and decisive action.

Moreover, disinformation fuels social division, exacerbating existing tensions within communities. When false narratives take flight, they can foster an "us versus them" mentality, leading to polarization on issues ranging from immigration to health care. Social media platforms, which were initially heralded as tools for democratizing information, have become breeding grounds for echo chambers, where misinformation is amplified and dissenting voices are drowned out. The ramifications are profound, as communities become fragmented, making it increasingly arduous to forge a collective understanding of the issues that affect us all.

Given the alarming trends surrounding disinformation and its effects on society, it becomes imperative to equip ourselves with the necessary tools to discern fact from fiction. The first step in this journey is to develop a critical mindset when consuming information. This means questioning the credibility of sources, seeking out multiple perspectives, and being vigilant about the motives behind the information we encounter.

One practical strategy is to verify the author and the publication before accepting any information as truth. Is the author an expert in their field? Does the publication have a reputation for journalistic integrity? Engaging with reliable sources is essential. Renowned fact-checking organizations such as Snopes, FactCheck.org, and the Poynter Institute provide accessible resources to help individuals navigate the murky waters of misinformation. These organizations employ rigorous methodologies to evaluate claims and dispel myths, serving as a bulwark against the tide of disinformation.

Next, online verification tools such as Google Reverse Image Search and TinEye can be invaluable in assessing the authenticity of images and videos that circulate widely on social media. The visual component of disinformation is particularly potent; a misleading image can spread like wildfire, often leaving a trail of misinformation in its wake. By utilizing these tools, individuals can trace the origins of images and ascertain their context, helping to curb the spread of false narratives.

Additionally, media literacy education emerges as a fundamental component of the toolkit for resisting disinformation. Schools, community organizations, and even families can play a pivotal role in fostering critical thinking skills among individuals, particularly the younger generation. Teaching children how to evaluate sources, discern biases, and seek out evidence instills habits that can carry through into adulthood, creating a more informed citizenry capable of navigating the complexities of modern media.

Active engagement with information is another cornerstone of resisting disinformation. It is all too easy to passively consume media, scrolling through feeds without questioning the veracity of the content we encounter. However, active engagement requires a shift in mindset—viewing ourselves not just as consumers of information but as critical thinkers and informed participants in the discourse surrounding the issues that matter.

Consider the story of a local activist who took it upon themselves to counter misinformation within their community. Faced with a wave of disinformation regarding a proposed public health initiative, they organized community forums to discuss the facts and debunk the false claims circulating on social media. By creating a space for dialogue and providing accurate information, they were able to mitigate fears and rebuild trust within their community. Their actions illustrate the power of engagement—not only in confronting disinformation but also in fostering a sense of community and informed citizenship.

Visual aids can also be potent tools for engagement. Infographics that distill complex information into digestible formats can serve as effective counterweights to the deluge of disinformation. For example, an infographic that compares scientific consensus on climate change to misinformation can clarify the reality of the situation for those who may be confused. Utilizing compelling visuals can capture attention and promote understanding, making it easier for people to engage meaningfully with important issues.

As we reflect on the profound implications of disinformation and the strategies for resisting it, it becomes clear that understanding and navigating this complex landscape is not merely an academic exercise; it is a civic duty. The importance of fostering informed citizenship cannot be overstated. Each person has a role to play in challenging manipulative narratives and supporting a more truthful discourse.

In conclusion, the battle against disinformation is one that requires vigilance, engagement, and a commitment to critical thinking. By assessing the impact of misinformation on public trust and democratic processes, we can better appreciate the urgency of the situation. Armed with practical strategies for discerning credible information, we can fortify ourselves against the tide of falsehood that seeks to undermine our collective understanding.

Empowerment lies in knowledge and action; by fostering a culture of informed discourse, we can reclaim the narrative from those who seek to manipulate it. It is imperative that we stand firm against disinformation, not only for our own sake but for the health of our communities and the integrity of our democratic institutions. In doing so, we pave the way for a more informed, united, and resilient society—one that values truth and holds fast to the principles of informed citizenship.

Chapter 11: Fostering Discord To Maintain Power

The concept of divide and rule, or as it has been known in various forms throughout history, has served as an effective mechanism for maintaining power and dominance over diverse populations. This strategy, deeply embedded in the fabric of political maneuvering, has often relied on the manipulation of fear, mistrust, and rivalries among different groups to prevent unity and foster discord. To understand the significance of divide and rule, one must first look into its definition and the psychological underpinnings that enable it to flourish across different contexts and times.

At its core, divide and rule is a political strategy used to gain and maintain control over a population by creating divisions among the subjects. Such divisions can be based on ethnicity, religion, social class, or any other salient identity factor that can be exploited. The objective is to prevent these groups from forming a cohesive front that could challenge the authority of those in power. By sowing discord, the ruling power can consolidate its position and maintain dominance, often at the expense of the very groups it manipulates.

The psychological mechanisms that underpin divide and rule tactics are crucial to understanding their effectiveness. Fear plays a pivotal role, as it is a powerful motivator for individuals and communities, often leading them to prioritize their own immediate safety over collective goals. Mistrust among groups can be amplified through carefully constructed narratives that highlight perceived threats from neighboring factions or communities. By fostering rivalries and competing interests, those in power can ensure that potential coalitions among the oppressed remain fragmented and ineffective.

As we traverse through history, the application of divide and rule strategies can be observed in various empires and regimes that sought to expand their influence and control. One of the earliest and most prominent examples is that of the Roman Empire, which, at its height, encompassed a vast array of cultures and peoples across Europe, North Africa, and parts of the Middle East. To manage such a diverse population, the Romans employed a variety of tactics designed to exploit local divisions.

The Roman Empire understood that maintaining order in such an expansive territory required more than just military might; it necessitated a nuanced approach that recognized and manipulated existing power dynamics within conquered societies. The Romans often co-opted local leaders, allowing them a degree of autonomy in exchange for loyalty to the empire. This method not only placated local populations but also created a hierarchy of power that ensured the Romans remained at the top.

Additionally, the Romans were adept at exploiting rivalries between different factions within these populations. By favoring one group over another, the empire could incite conflict among local factions, distracting them from potential rebellion against Roman authority. This strategy was evident in regions such as Gaul, where the Romans played various Gallic tribes against one another, ensuring that no single tribe could amass enough power to challenge Roman rule. The resultant fragmentation created a scenario wherein the various tribes remained focused on their rivalries, allowing the Romans to maintain control with minimal military intervention.

Transitioning from the ancient practices of the Romans, we observe similar divide and rule strategies being employed during the era of the British Empire, particularly throughout its colonial endeavors. The British were notorious for their ability to exploit ethnic and social divisions within the territories they colonized, utilizing these fractures to solidify their own power and authority.

A prime example of this can be seen in British India, where the colonial administration capitalized on the existing religious and ethnic divides between Hindus and Muslims. Through a combination of policies that favored certain groups over others and a campaign of divide and conquer, the British were able to instigate tensions that would ultimately lead to communal violence and discord. The British policy of "divide and rule" not only served to maintain their control but also left lasting scars on the social fabric of India, creating divisions that would continue to resonate long after colonialism had ended.

The impact of these tactics was profound. In many instances, the colonial powers implemented systems of governance that entrenched these divisions, creating lasting consequences that would shape post-colonial societies. For instance, the 1947 partition of India, which resulted in the creation of Pakistan, is often cited as a direct result of the divisive policies instituted by the British. This catastrophic event, marked by massive population displacement and widespread violence, highlighted the long-term ramifications of divide and rule strategies, as communities that had coexisted for centuries found themselves pitted against one another in a newly defined landscape of rivalry and suspicion.

Beyond the Roman and British Empires, one can observe other historical examples where divide and rule strategies have been employed effectively. The Ottoman Empire, for instance, utilized a system known as the millet system, which allowed various religious and ethnic groups to maintain a degree of autonomy under the overarching authority of the empire. While this approach brought some measure of stability, it also reinforced divisions among the populations, as each group became more entrenched in its own identity and less inclined to collaborate with others.

Similarly, in the context of French colonialism, particularly in North Africa, the French implemented policies that privileged certain ethnic groups over others, resulting in a cascade of riots and unrest fueled by resentment among those who were marginalized. By creating a hierarchy among the colonized populations, the French were able to suppress potential uprisings, yet these decisions precipitated a legacy of division that would haunt the region for generations.

As we consider the evolution of divide and rule strategies, it becomes evident that these tactics have not remained static; rather, they have adapted over time to reflect changing political landscapes. The methods employed by ancient empires have transformed dramatically, yet the core principle remains the same: to exploit divisions to maintain control. In modern contexts, we see a shift from overt military coercion to more insidious forms of manipulation that exploit social media, misinformation, and propaganda to foster division.

The contemporary landscape is marked by a significant transition in how divide and rule is enacted. Where once physical presence and military might were required to maintain dominance, today, the advent of technology has allowed for more subtle approaches. Governments and political actors can manipulate narratives and sow discord among populations from a distance, using online platforms to amplify fears and mistrust. Social media has become a potent tool for spreading misinformation, enabling the creation of echo chambers that reinforce existing biases while further entrenching divisions.

The psychological principles that underlie divide and rule strategies remain relevant, with fear and mistrust continuing to play pivotal roles in shaping group dynamics. As political entities leverage these emotions, they cultivate an environment where individuals are more likely to retreat into their own identities rather than engage with others. Propaganda, whether through traditional media or modern digital platforms, serves to reinforce these divisions, creating a landscape where individuals are often pitted against one another based on manipulated narratives.

In conclusion, the exploration of divide and rule strategies reveals a complex interplay of historical, psychological, and political factors that have shaped societies across time. From the Roman Empire to contemporary political landscapes, these tactics have evolved yet maintained their core objective: to fracture potential coalitions among diverse groups to sustain power. As we transition into a discussion of the contemporary relevance of these strategies, it is imperative to recognize that the lessons from history offer critical insights into our present and future political dynamics. Understanding the historical context and evolution of divide and rule strategies equips us to confront the challenges posed by these tactics in our increasingly interconnected world.

The concept of divide and rule has undergone a significant evolution in the contemporary landscape, particularly influenced by the advent and proliferation of social media. As platforms like Facebook, Twitter, Instagram, and TikTok have integrated themselves into the very fabric of daily life, divisive narratives have found fertile ground to grow. Political leaders, corporations, and various interest groups have harnessed these platforms, employing age-old strategies of division to consolidate power and control. Yet, amidst these developments, a counter-movement has emerged, leveraging the same tools to foster unity and resistance against the tides of division. This subchapter will explore contemporary examples of the divide and rule strategy, the role of social media in perpetuating and resisting these tactics, and the critical engagement necessary for individuals to navigate this complex terrain.

In the realm of contemporary politics, division has become a cornerstone strategy for many leaders seeking to consolidate power. The rise of identity politics has been particularly significant in recent years, with political figures often capitalizing on societal divides to galvanize support. The 2016

United States presidential election serves as a prime example. Candidates utilized rhetoric that appealed to specific demographics, creating a narrative that pitted groups against each other. The election not only highlighted the polarization within American society but also illustrated how political leaders could employ divisive strategies to energize their bases. The phrase "Make America Great Again," for instance, invoked feelings of nostalgia while simultaneously suggesting that certain groups were responsible for the nation's perceived decline, thereby deepening existing divides.

In various parts of the world, similar tactics have been observed. In Brazil, the 2018 presidential election saw Jair Bolsonaro rise to power through a campaign that emphasized law and order, appealing to citizens' fears regarding crime and corruption. By framing the political landscape as a battleground between "good" citizens and "criminal" elements, Bolsonaro effectively divided the electorate along social, economic, and racial lines. This strategy not only helped him secure a substantial following but also fostered an atmosphere of hostility toward opponents, further entrenching societal divisions.

Beyond politics, corporate influence has also played a pivotal role in exploiting social divides for profit and control. Companies often capitalize on cultural, racial, and economic disparities to market their products, effectively deepening the divides they purport to bridge. For instance, brands may create marketing campaigns that specifically target marginalized communities, suggesting that purchasing their products is a means of empowerment. While such strategies may appear innocuous or even progressive on the surface, they can serve to commodify and exploit social identities, perpetuating the very divisions they aim to tap into.

Social media has emerged as both a catalyst for division and a platform for resistance. The complexities of these platforms have enabled the rapid dissemination of divisive narratives, often magnified by algorithms designed to promote engagement over accuracy. Content that elicits strong emotional reactions—whether outrage, fear, or excitement—is more likely to be shared and circulated widely, creating a feedback loop that reinforces existing biases and splits communities.

Algorithms on platforms like Facebook and Twitter often prioritize content that generates high levels of engagement, inadvertently promoting divisive content. Studies have shown that sensational narratives and misinformation spread faster than factual reporting, creating echo chambers where individuals are continually exposed to similar viewpoints. These echo chambers not only validate existing beliefs but also contribute to an increasingly polarized society, making it challenging for individuals to encounter differing perspectives.

The phenomenon of misinformation further exacerbates this issue. False narratives can easily be disseminated through social media, leading to significant misunderstandings and heightened tensions among different groups. The COVID-19 pandemic provided fertile ground for misinformation to thrive, with various narratives about the virus creating divisions over how to respond to the public health crisis. Misinformation about vaccines, for instance, became a flashpoint for conflict, with social media platforms serving as conduits for both the spread of false information and the mobilization of anti-vaccine movements.

However, social media is not solely a tool for division; it also serves as a platform for resistance and unity. Grassroots movements have harnessed the power of these digital platforms to promote collective action and foster solidarity among diverse groups. Movements such as Black Lives Matter have gained international traction through social media, utilizing hashtags, viral campaigns, and online activism to draw attention to systemic injustices and galvanize support for change.

The success of such movements illustrates the potential for social media to unite individuals across geographic, racial, and socio-economic divides, counteracting the divisive narratives perpetuated by those in power. For example, during the protests following the murder of George Floyd in 2020, social media played a crucial role in mobilizing individuals from various backgrounds to participate in demonstrations and advocate for justice.

The #BlackLivesMatter hashtag became a rallying cry, transcending geographic boundaries and fostering a sense of solidarity among activists worldwide.

The counter-narratives created by these grassroots movements serve as a powerful reminder that social media can be wielded as a tool for promoting unity and collective action in the face of divisiveness. Campaigns advocating for social justice, climate action, and human rights have successfully harnessed the connectivity offered by these platforms, demonstrating the potential for digital activism to effect meaningful change at local, national, and global levels.

Yet, the challenge remains for individuals to engage critically with the information they encounter on social media. In an era characterized by misinformation and polarization, it is essential for users to develop the skills necessary to analyze and question the narratives presented to them. This requires an active engagement with content, seeking out multiple perspectives, and being discerning about sources of information.

One effective strategy for identifying divisive narratives is to consider the motivations behind the content being shared. Are the authors attempting to evoke fear or anger? Are they framing a situation in a way that pits one group against another? Such questions can help individuals recognize when they are being manipulated by divisive tactics. Additionally, fostering open dialogue with others who hold differing views can provide opportunities for understanding and bridging divides, transforming social media into a space for constructive discourse rather than conflict.

In conclusion, the modern applications of divide and rule strategies and the resistance against them in the age of social media underscore the complexities of our digital landscape. Political leaders and corporations increasingly exploit social divides for power and profit, leading to a fragmented society characterized by polarization and conflict. However, the same platforms that facilitate division also serve as a battleground for grassroots movements advocating for unity and social justice. The challenge for individuals lies in critically engaging with the information they encounter, actively seeking to understand the narratives that shape their perspectives, and fostering dialogue with those who hold different views.

As we navigate this complex terrain, informed citizenship becomes paramount in combating the divide and rule strategy. By promoting understanding, solidarity, and critical engagement, individuals can contribute to a more equitable and united society, challenging the narratives that seek to divide us.

12.1 Understanding Cognitive Biases and Their Role in Propaganda

Imagine scrolling through your social media feed, only to stumble upon a sensational headline that screams for your attention: "New Study Finds 90% of Scientists Agree: Climate Change is the End of Us!" Accompanying this bold statement is a striking image of a melting iceberg, an emotional appeal that plays on the viewer's fears. As you read through the comments, you notice a mix of outrage and agreement, with users vehemently taking sides. In this scenario, emotions run high, and judgment becomes clouded, but what's happening underneath the surface? This is a prime example of how cognitive biases can color our interpretations of information, often leading us to conclusions that may not be entirely rational.

Cognitive biases are systematic patterns of deviation from norm or rationality in judgment. They often arise from our brain's attempts to simplify information processing, making it easier to navigate a complex world. However, these shortcuts can lead us astray, particularly when we are confronted with emotionally charged narratives, such as those often found in propaganda. Understanding the nuances of cognitive biases equips us with a critical lens to examine the information we consume, particularly in an age where misinformation proliferates at an unprecedented rate.

One of the most pervasive cognitive biases is confirmation bias, a tendency to search for, interpret, and remember information in a way that confirms one's preexisting beliefs. This bias can manifest in various forms, such as selectively gathering evidence that supports a particular viewpoint while discounting opposing evidence. A landmark study conducted by social psychologist Wason in the 1960s demonstrated this phenomenon through a simple card selection task. Participants were presented with a set of cards and tasked with determining a rule. Most participants only selected cards that would confirm their hypothesis, rather than seeking evidence that could potentially disprove it. This demonstrates a significant reluctance to engage with information that contradicts one's beliefs, which can lead to entrenched viewpoints and polarized opinions.

To illustrate the implications of confirmation bias in a real-world context, consider the landscape of online news consumption. Research has shown that individuals often curate their news feeds to reflect their existing beliefs, following sources that reinforce their perspectives while avoiding those that challenge them. This behavior is particularly evident in politically charged environments, where individuals gravitate toward news outlets that align with their ideological orientations. For example, during the 2016 U.S. presidential election, studies revealed that supporters of Donald Trump primarily consumed media that portrayed him in a favorable light, while those who supported Hillary Clinton sought out information that aligned with their views. This selective exposure not only bolsters confirmation bias but also exacerbates societal divisions, as individuals become increasingly insulated in their echo chambers.

Another significant cognitive bias is the anchoring bias, which refers to the human tendency to rely too heavily on the first piece of information encountered when making decisions. This initial information serves as a mental "anchor" that influences subsequent judgments and interpretations. For instance, if a person hears that a new smartphone has a starting price of $999, their perception of what constitutes a reasonable price for a smartphone may be skewed, even if they later encounter models priced lower. This bias underscores the importance of the framing and presentation of information, as it can shape our understanding and expectations.

A compelling example of anchoring bias in action can be seen in the marketing strategies employed by various industries. Consider a luxury car brand that advertises a new model with a prominently displayed MSRP (Manufacturer's Suggested Retail Price) of $70,000. Even if the final sale price is subsequently negotiated down to $60,000, potential buyers may perceive this deal as highly favorable because their perception was initially anchored to the higher price. In this context, the initial pricing serves as a reference point that can skew their perception of value, demonstrating the profound impact of anchoring on consumer behavior.

The bandwagon effect, another cognitive bias, reflects the tendency for individuals to adopt certain behaviors or beliefs simply because others are doing so. This phenomenon often leads to a snowballing effect in public opinion, where the popularity of a viewpoint can create a perception of validity. As more people express support for a particular position, others may feel compelled to join in, driven by the fear of exclusion or the desire for social validation.

A notorious example of the bandwagon effect can be observed during election cycles, where candidates' popularity can shift dramatically based on perceptions of their standing in the polls. For instance, during the 2008 United States presidential election, Barack Obama initially struggled to gain traction against Hillary Clinton in the Democratic primary. However, as he began to receive significant media coverage and garnered endorsements from key figures, public support began to snowball. The perception of Obama as a viable candidate led more individuals to back him, not necessarily due to a change in beliefs but rather from a desire to align with the perceived winner. This phenomenon illustrates how susceptibility to social pressures can influence individual choices, further complicating the landscape of public opinion.

Understanding these cognitive biases is crucial when examining the impact of propaganda on society. Individuals often embrace propaganda uncritically, swayed by the emotional appeals and selective narratives that align with their cognitive predispositions. Propagandists are keenly aware of these biases, and they craft their messages with precision to exploit them. By appealing to confirmation bias, for instance, they may present information that resonates with preexisting beliefs, thereby fostering a sense of validation among their target audience.

Research has illuminated the insidious nature of cognitive biases in relation to misinformation and propaganda. A study published in the journal "Psychological Science" revealed that individuals exposed to false information were more likely to retain those inaccuracies when they aligned with their beliefs, regardless of subsequent corrections. This tendency underscores the challenges of combating misinformation; once a belief is formed, it can be incredibly resistant to revision, even in the face of compelling evidence.

Moreover, cognitive biases contribute to the phenomenon of "fake news" becoming entrenched in public discourse. Individuals who encounter sensational headlines or misleading information may be more inclined to share that content, particularly if it aligns with their views. This sharing behavior can further perpetuate misinformation, creating an environment where false narratives thrive, often leading to a distorted understanding of critical issues.

In conclusion, cognitive biases play a pivotal role in shaping our perceptions and interpretations of information, particularly in the realm of propaganda. By understanding these biases, we can develop a more critical approach to the information we consume, allowing us to navigate the complexities of modern discourse with greater discernment. As we strive to cultivate informed opinions, recognizing the influence of emotional triggers and cognitive shortcuts can empower us to confront misinformation head-on, ultimately fostering a more informed and discerning society. In an age where propaganda is intricately woven into the fabric of our media landscape, the ability to critically evaluate information has never been more essential.

In the intricate dance of human communication and persuasion, the interplay between psychological principles and the art of propaganda is a phenomenon that has persisted through the ages. In our modern landscape, where information is abundant yet scrutinized, understanding these principles is not just an academic pursuit; it is an essential skill for navigating the complexities of contemporary discourse. The adage that knowledge is power rings particularly true in this context, as we strive to equip ourselves with the tools necessary for critical engagement.

One of the most salient psychological principles underpinning propaganda is the framing effect. This concept elucidates how the presentation of information can significantly shape our perceptions and interpretations. The framing effect hinges on the idea that the context in which information is delivered can lead to vastly different responses, even when the underlying facts remain unchanged. To illustrate this, consider the strategic framing employed during a political campaign. Imagine two candidates vying for the same office—one framed as a "political outsider" championing change, while the other is depicted as a "career politician" entrenched in the status quo. The implications of such framing are profound; the first candidate may gain favor among voters seeking innovation, while the latter may be viewed with skepticism and distrust.

A striking case study that exemplifies the effectiveness of the framing effect is the 2008 presidential campaign of Barack Obama. The campaign masterfully harnessed the power of positive framing, positioning Obama as a beacon of hope and change in stark contrast to the perceived failures of the previous administration. This strategic framing not only galvanized support among younger voters but also helped to define the narrative surrounding the election. The use of uplifting imagery, evocative language, and a compelling vision of the future effectively reframed the political landscape, allowing Obama to resonate with the public on an emotional level and ultimately secure victory.

In addition to framing, the principles of social proof and authority play pivotal roles in propagandistic messaging. Human beings are inherently social creatures, often looking to others to guide their beliefs and behaviors. This tendency is amplified in times of uncertainty, where individuals may seek validation from credible figures or groups.

The concept of social proof posits that people are more likely to adopt beliefs or engage in behaviors that they observe others endorsing, particularly when those others are perceived as authoritative or expert in a given domain.

Consider the realm of advertising, where brands frequently leverage authority figures to endorse their products. A well-known example is the use of athletes in commercial campaigns. When a celebrated athlete promotes a sports drink, consumers are more likely to trust the product's efficacy, influenced by the athlete's expertise and status. Similarly, in the political sphere, endorsements from influential figures can sway public opinion substantially. A prominent politician or celebrity publicly supporting a candidate can enhance that candidate's credibility and attractiveness in the eyes of potential voters.

As we look deeper into the realm of propaganda, it becomes increasingly evident that emotional appeals serve as a powerful weapon in the arsenal of persuasion. The manipulation of emotions can often bypass rational scrutiny, rendering individuals vulnerable to influence. Propagandists are well aware that emotions such as fear, anger, and patriotism can evoke visceral responses that cloud judgment and prompt action, often without thorough consideration of the underlying facts.

Historically, wartime propaganda provides some of the most poignant examples of emotional manipulation. During World War I and World War II, governments employed fear-inducing imagery and rhetoric to galvanize support for the war effort. Posters depicting the enemy as monstrous threats to national security incited fear and spurred enlistment, while appeals to patriotism urged citizens to contribute to the war financially, often at great personal sacrifice. The visceral imagery and emotionally charged language employed in these campaigns created a sense of urgency and necessity, compelling individuals to act in the name of national pride and survival.

In the contemporary media landscape, emotional appeals continue to thrive, albeit in different forms. News outlets and social media platforms often sensationalize events to provoke outrage or indignation, drawing viewers and readers into a cycle of heightened emotional engagement. The proliferation of clickbait headlines and attention-grabbing visuals serves to escalate the emotional stakes, often overshadowing the critical analysis of issues at hand. For instance, a news story that emphasizes violent protests or civil unrest may invoke a sense of fear and helplessness, prompting viewers to react instinctively rather than thoughtfully engage with the complexities of the situation.

In light of the powerful psychological influences at play, it becomes imperative for individuals to cultivate a toolkit of strategies aimed at identifying and countering these effects. Recognizing the tendency to fall prey to emotional manipulation and social influences is the first step toward fostering critical engagement. Self-reflection is a powerful ally in this endeavor; individuals must take the time to examine their own biases and preconceptions, striving to understand how these factors may color their interpretations of information.

Moreover, fostering an environment that encourages critical

thinking and informed discussions within communities is essential. This can be achieved through open dialogues that prioritize active listening and respectful debate. Engaging with diverse perspectives not only broadens one's understanding but also strengthens the ability to discern credible information from misleading narratives. Educational initiatives that emphasize media literacy can empower individuals to navigate the complexities of information consumption, equipping them with the skills necessary to analyze sources critically and recognize manipulative tactics.

As we arrive at the conclusion of this exploration into the psychological underpinnings of propaganda, it is vital to reiterate the significance of understanding these principles as we engage with the world around us. By cultivating an awareness of framing effects, social proof, emotional manipulation, and our own biases, we position ourselves to become informed citizens capable of navigating the murky waters of modern discourse.

The call to action is clear: we must approach information critically, engaging thoughtfully with the narratives that shape our understanding of the world. By embracing the principles of critical engagement outlined in this subchapter, we not only enhance our own ability to think independently but also contribute to the cultivation of a more informed and discerning society. The power of knowledge is indeed profound, and as we harness this power, we take essential strides toward becoming proactive participants in the democratic process, ensuring that our voices are informed by clarity rather than clutter, by understanding rather than ignorance. Through this lens, we can aspire to foster a culture of critical engagement that transcends the limitations of propaganda, enabling us to construct a more nuanced and comprehensive understanding of the intricate tapestry of human communication.

In the intricate dance of communication, where messages are crafted, shaped, and delivered with strategic intent, cognitive biases emerge as pivotal actors in how individuals decode and respond to information. At their core, cognitive biases are systematic patterns of deviation from norm or rationality in judgment, a kind of mental shortcut that can help streamline our decision-making processes. However, these biases often lead to perceptual distortions, inaccurate judgments, illogical interpretations, or what can be broadly understood as a warped view of reality. As individuals navigate through the cacophony of information in the contemporary world, particularly in the context of propaganda, recognizing and understanding these biases becomes crucial—not merely for personal insight but for informed citizenship in an increasingly complex socio-political landscape.

The relevance of cognitive biases to propaganda is profound. Propaganda, a tool often wielded for persuasion, manipulation, or ideological indoctrination, exploits these innate psychological quirks to achieve its ends. By understanding cognitive biases, we can gain insights into why certain messages resonate more than others and why individuals may gravitate towards information that aligns with their preconceived beliefs while dismissing contradictory perspectives. Through this lens, biases are not merely obstacles to rational thought; they are foundational elements that underpin our interactions with information, shaping our opinions and influencing our affiliations.

To fully grasp this relationship, it is essential to look into some of the key cognitive biases that are especially relevant in the context of propaganda. Among these biases, confirmation bias stands out prominently. Defined as the tendency to search for, interpret, favor, and recall information in a way that confirms one's preexisting beliefs or hypotheses, confirmation bias acts as a powerful filter for how we engage with data and narratives. In practical terms, this means that individuals are more likely to notice and give weight to information that aligns with their beliefs, while conveniently overlooking or outright rejecting information that contradicts them.

A vivid real-world example of confirmation bias can be seen in the political arena, particularly during election campaigns. In today's hyper-connected world, social media platforms serve as fertile grounds for this bias to flourish. Political campaigns often tailor their messaging to resonate with specific voter demographics, exploiting existing beliefs and sentiments. Within this environment, echo chambers emerge—online spaces where individuals interact primarily with like-minded individuals, amplifying their views while marginalizing dissent. Here, confirmation bias operates seamlessly, as individuals actively seek out information that validates their political opinions, bolstering their support for candidates or policies. This self-reinforcing cycle can lead to an increasingly polarized electorate, where the very foundation of democratic discourse becomes threatened by a lack of exposure to diverse viewpoints.

Another critical cognitive bias that plays a vital role in the effectiveness of propaganda is the illusory truth effect. This phenomenon refers to the tendency to believe information to be true after repeated exposure, regardless of its actual veracity. When people encounter a statement multiple times, their familiarity with the assertion can create a false sense of truthfulness. This bias is particularly salient in an age where misinformation can be disseminated rapidly, often across multiple platforms and channels, leading to widespread acceptance of inaccuracies.

A particularly relevant instance of the illusory truth effect can be observed in the realm of misinformation campaigns. Consider, for example, the proliferation of false information regarding health practices during a public health crisis. As various narratives emerge, repeated exposure to misleading claims can lead individuals to accept those claims as factual, regardless of the scientific evidence that contradicts them. This acceptance can have serious consequences, influencing individual behaviors and public policy. The illusory truth effect underscores the importance of media literacy and critical thinking in an era where the truth can be obscured by repetition and emotional appeal—a hallmark of effective propaganda.

The bandwagon effect represents yet another cognitive bias that is instrumental in understanding how propaganda can sway public opinion. This bias reflects the propensity to adopt certain behaviors, follow trends, or purchase items primarily because others are doing so. It is the psychological underpinning of the saying "if everyone is doing it, it must be right." When individuals perceive that a belief or action is popular or widely accepted, they are more inclined to embrace it, often without critically evaluating the underlying merits or evidence.

In the context of social movements, the bandwagon effect can lead to rapid shifts in public opinion. For instance, consider a popular social cause gaining traction through media coverage and celebrity endorsements. As more individuals express support for the cause, others may feel compelled to join in, not necessarily because they have formed a well-reasoned stance, but rather due to the social validation they perceive in the collective action of others. This phenomenon reinforces the power of propaganda in shaping societal norms and catalyzing change, particularly when individuals prioritize social acceptance over independent judgment.

The combined influence of these cognitive biases—confirmation bias, the illusory truth effect, and the bandwagon effect—illustrates a critical vulnerability in human cognition that propagandists exploit to their advantage. By crafting messages that align with existing beliefs, repetitively disseminating information, and leveraging social dynamics, propagandists can effectively sway public opinion and alter perceptions. The susceptibility to these biases highlights the need for individuals to cultivate a critical mindset, to question the information they consume, and to seek out diverse perspectives that challenge their preconceived notions.

Recognizing cognitive biases is not merely an intellectual exercise; it serves as a crucial component of effective critical thinking. By understanding how these biases operate, individuals can develop the skills necessary to navigate the complex landscape of modern information. This awareness can empower individuals to scrutinize sources, challenge prevailing narratives, and engage in informed discussions. In doing so, they can counteract the pernicious effects of propaganda and make decisions that align with their values and beliefs rather than those that have been artificially constructed through manipulative messaging.

In conclusion, the exploration of cognitive biases provides invaluable insights into the psychological mechanisms that underlie human perception and decision-making in the face of propaganda. By unraveling how biases like confirmation bias, the illusory truth effect, and the bandwagon effect function, readers gain a deeper understanding of their own vulnerabilities when confronted with persuasive messaging. This knowledge not only fosters critical thinking but also equips individuals with the tools necessary to navigate an increasingly complex information landscape. As we transition into the next chapter, which will look into various propaganda techniques, we will build upon this foundational understanding, exploring how these biases are systematically exploited to shape public opinion and alter societal narratives. Armed with this knowledge, we can better prepare ourselves to engage thoughtfully and critically with the world around us.

In our rapidly evolving information landscape, where the boundaries between fact and fiction often blur, understanding the complex interplay between cognitive biases and propaganda techniques becomes not only relevant but crucial. The bombardment of information that we experience daily varies greatly in quality, truthfulness, and intent. Many of us find ourselves navigating this tumultuous environment, often unaware of the subtle mechanisms at play that can manipulate our perceptions and beliefs. At the heart of this manipulation lies propaganda—an age-old tactic that skilled communicators exploit to sway public opinion, incite emotions, or champion specific agendas.

Propaganda is not merely the dissemination of misleading information; it is a sophisticated art that operates on the fundamental principles of human psychology. Cognitive biases—systematic patterns of deviation from norm or rationality in judgment—serve as fertile ground for these propaganda techniques. They exploit our shortcuts in processing information, our tendency to favor information that aligns with our preexisting beliefs, and our emotional responses. As we look into the nuances of propaganda techniques, we will uncover their connections to cognitive biases and highlight the importance of recognizing these techniques, particularly in the context of pervasive misinformation that permeates our social discourse.

Understanding propaganda is not just about identifying what is false; it is also about developing the tools to discern the motivations behind various messages and how they may seek to influence our thoughts and actions. The stakes in this endeavor are immense. With the proliferation of digital media, the channels through which propaganda is disseminated have expanded dramatically. As we engage more frequently with online platforms, where sensationalized headlines and emotionally charged content vie for our attention, equipping ourselves with knowledge becomes an act of agency. It empowers us to sift through the noise and engage with information critically, making informed decisions based on a foundation of solid evidence rather than emotional manipulation.

As we explore the key propaganda techniques that harness cognitive biases, we will begin with emotional appeal. This technique is powerful because it speaks directly to our feelings—fear, joy, anger, and pride—and often bypasses rational scrutiny.

Emotional appeal prompts us to react instinctively, leading us to make judgments based on our feelings rather than objective analysis.

A classic example of emotional appeal can be found in wartime propaganda posters, which evoke strong feelings of fear or patriotism to galvanize public support. During World War II, for instance, many countries employed vivid imagery and emotive slogans to encourage enlistment and rally support for war efforts. The iconic "Uncle Sam Wants You" poster, with its stark imagery and direct call to action, tapped into a sense of duty and national pride. Similarly, posters depicting the enemy in grotesque, dehumanizing ways played on fears about invasion and loss, prompting viewers to react emotionally rather than rationally.

The effectiveness of emotional appeals cannot be overstated. They engage our primal instincts and compel us to act in ways that we might not otherwise consider. This technique thrives on our cognitive biases, particularly the availability heuristic, where we judge the likelihood of events based on how easily examples come to mind. If we are repeatedly exposed to emotionally charged narratives, they become ingrained in our psyche, shaping our perceptions and potentially leading to oversimplified conclusions about complex issues.

Another prevalent propaganda technique is repetition. Repetition serves to reinforce messages, making them more memorable and believable. This technique operates on the principle that familiarity breeds acceptance; the more we hear something, the more likely we are to believe it, regardless of its truthfulness. Political advertising frequently utilizes repetition to great effect. Candidates often recite key phrases or slogans throughout their campaigns, embedding these messages in the public consciousness. For instance, during election cycles, we often hear candidates repeating their core messages—"Make America Great Again" or "Yes We Can"—to solidify their platforms in the minds of voters.

The impact of repeated messaging is profound. A study from the University of California found that individuals exposed to repeated false information were more likely to believe it, regardless of whether they initially held a different view. This phenomenon, sometimes referred to as the illusory truth effect, highlights how repetition can distort our understanding of reality, leading us to accept unverified claims as fact simply due to their frequency in our daily encounters.

Social proof is yet another technique that propagandists exploit, leveraging our inherent desire to conform to the actions of others. This cognitive bias manifests when we look to others for cues on how to behave, especially in ambiguous situations. Misinformation campaigns on social media perfectly illustrate this technique, as false information spreads virally when individuals see their peers engage with it. The more people share a particular narrative or statistic, the more it appears valid to others, creating an echo chamber that reinforces the falsehood.

A notable example of social proof can be observed during the COVID-19 pandemic, where misinformation about the virus, its origins, and treatment options proliferated across social media platforms. False claims about unproven remedies gained traction not only because they were shared extensively but also because individuals observed friends and family engaging with the content. The viral nature of misinformation exploits our cognitive biases, leading us to question valid, evidence-based information while simultaneously accepting dubious claims.

The implications of these propaganda techniques and their exploitation of cognitive biases extend beyond individual belief systems; they can shape public opinion and influence behavior on a grand scale. Historical case studies reveal instances where propaganda techniques have notably shifted societal norms or mobilized populations towards particular ends. During the Civil Rights Movement, propaganda played a significant role in changing perceptions about race and equality in the United States. The photographs and news coverage highlighting the brutality faced by civil rights activists served as a catalyst for widespread public outrage. Here, emotional appeal not only informed public opinion but also led to tangible changes in laws and societal norms.

In examining these case studies, it becomes evident that our susceptibility to propaganda is not merely a reflection of individual failures in judgment but rather a systemic issue that reflects the environment in which we consume information. The implications are profound: when cognitive biases and propaganda techniques intertwine, public discourse can be dangerously skewed, resulting in division, misinformation, and a breakdown of trust in institutions.

To navigate this complex landscape, it is essential to develop strategies for recognizing and resisting propaganda. Awareness is the first step; understanding the techniques employed can empower us to discern when we are being manipulated.

One practical strategy is fact-checking and verifying sources before accepting information as truth. In an age where misinformation spreads like wildfire, taking the time to consult reputable sources can make a significant difference. Websites like Snopes, FactCheck.org, or the Poynter Institute provide valuable resources for checking the veracity of claims. While this might seem tedious, especially when confronted with the immediacy of social media, it is a non-negotiable step in the quest for accurate information.

Beyond verification, seeking diverse perspectives is crucial for developing a well-rounded understanding of any issue. Engaging with a variety of sources—both those that align with our views and those that challenge them—fosters critical thinking and helps guard against the echo chamber effect. In doing so, we cultivate the ability to appreciate differing viewpoints, leading to more nuanced discussions that move beyond binary understandings.

Recognizing emotional manipulation is another essential skill in resisting propaganda. Understanding how emotions can skew our perception of facts can help us step back and analyze information more critically. When we encounter a message that elicits a strong emotional response, taking a moment to assess its content and context is essential. What are the underlying assumptions? Whom does it serve? By interrogating emotionally charged content, we can mitigate the risk of making impulsive judgments based solely on how we feel.

As we reflect on the significance of understanding propaganda techniques, it becomes clear that knowledge is not merely a tool but a form of empowerment. The ability to discern fact from fiction enriches our engagement with the world. We must take responsibility for our media consumption, recognizing that we have the agency to shape our beliefs and, ultimately, our actions.

In a society inundated with information, the responsibility lies with each of us to engage as informed citizens. As we become more attuned to the techniques that seek to manipulate our thoughts, we can advocate for greater transparency in communication, demand accountability from those who disseminate information, and foster a culture of critical engagement.

Ultimately, navigating a world rife with propaganda requires vigilance, curiosity, and a commitment to understanding the complexities of human cognition and communication. By equipping ourselves with the knowledge and strategies necessary to counteract these influences, we not only protect ourselves from manipulation but can also contribute to the collective effort of fostering a more informed, empathetic, and discerning society.

They're Lying to You

Chapter 12: Understanding Cognitive Biases in Propaganda

In the intricate landscape of human thought and behavior, cognitive biases serve as silent architects, subtly shaping our perceptions and choices, often without our conscious awareness. These biases, deeply embedded in our psychological framework, not only influence our day-to-day decisions but also play a pivotal role in how we interpret information—especially when it comes to propaganda. Understanding these cognitive biases is crucial in a world inundated with information, where the line between truth and manipulation can be alarmingly thin.

Cognitive biases can be understood as systematic patterns of deviation from norm or rationality in judgment. They arise from the brain's attempt to simplify information processing and are an inherent part of the human experience. For instance, when confronted with overwhelming data or complex situations, our brains often resort to mental shortcuts, leading us to conclusions that may feel comfortable or familiar, but are not necessarily accurate. This propensity to favor certain types of information over others can have profound implications for our decision-making processes.

To illustrate the significance of cognitive biases, consider the historical example of the 1938 War of the Worlds radio broadcast. On that fateful night, Orson Welles narrated an adaptation of H.G. Wells' science fiction novel, leading many listeners to believe that Earth was under attack from Martians. The ensuing panic was fueled by confirmation bias; many listeners sought information that confirmed their apprehensions about the world, dismissing the broadcast's disclaimers as irrelevant or untrustworthy. This incident not only highlights how cognitive biases can cloud judgment but also underscores the power of media in swaying public perception, an element that remains relevant today in the realm of propaganda.

As we look deeper into the various cognitive biases that underpin our interactions with propaganda, it becomes essential to explore their mechanisms and implications. Foremost among these biases is confirmation bias, a deeply ingrained tendency that significantly impacts how we process information and make decisions.

Confirmation bias is defined as the inclination to search for, interpret, favor, and recall information in a way that confirms one's preexisting beliefs or hypotheses. This cognitive bias can lead individuals to disregard evidence that contradicts their views, resulting in a distorted understanding of reality. For instance, during election cycles, voters often gravitate toward news sources and social media platforms that echo their political beliefs, filtering out dissenting opinions and information that challenges their viewpoints.

One powerful example of confirmation bias in action can be observed in the realm of conflicting news stories related to public health. During the COVID-19 pandemic, for instance, individuals with strong beliefs about vaccine efficacy often sought out information that supported their position, while simultaneously dismissing credible sources that presented counter-arguments regarding vaccine safety or effectiveness. This selective exposure can create echo chambers, where individuals reinforce their beliefs without engagement with opposing perspectives, thereby deepening societal divisions.

A particularly illustrative case study of this phenomenon occurred during the early stages of the pandemic, when public reaction to the information disseminated about mask-wearing fluctuated dramatically. Many individuals relied on their preexisting beliefs about government authority and personal freedoms, leading to polarized responses. For those who believed in the necessity of health mandates, data supporting mask-wearing was readily accepted, whereas for skeptics, dissenting views were amplified, often leading to public protests against mask mandates. This divergence in information processing not only affected individual decisions but also shaped broader societal responses to public health initiatives.

Another cognitive bias closely intertwined with the dynamics of propaganda is the bandwagon effect, a psychological phenomenon where individuals align their beliefs and behaviors with those of a larger group. The bandwagon effect underscores the social implications of decision-making, as people tend to adopt certain attitudes or actions simply because they perceive them to be popular or widely accepted. This tendency is particularly pronounced during political campaigns, where candidates and their supporters strategically leverage the bandwagon effect to gain traction and influence public opinion.

In the realm of political discourse, the bandwagon effect can manifest in various ways, such as endorsements from celebrities or influential figures, which serve to validate a candidate's appeal. For example, during the 2008 U.S. presidential election, Barack Obama's campaign skillfully harnessed the power of the bandwagon effect by presenting a narrative of hope and change that resonated widely, encouraging supporters to feel as though they were part of a larger, inclusive movement. The campaign's visuals, messaging, and grassroots mobilization efforts fostered a sense of belonging among voters, prompting many to join the "bandwagon" of support, often swaying undecided voters in the process.

Statistical data reinforces the presence of the bandwagon effect in electoral contexts. A study conducted by researchers at the University of California found that individuals exposed to a campaign message that highlighted its popularity were significantly more likely to express support for that campaign than those who received neutral or negative information. This dynamic reflects how perceptions of social consensus can have a profound influence on individual choices, further complicating the landscape of democratic decision-making.

To understand these cognitive biases fully, we must also explore the anchoring effect, a cognitive bias whereby individuals rely heavily on the first piece of information encountered when making decisions. This initial information acts as an "anchor," influencing subsequent judgments and evaluations, even if it is unrelated or irrelevant. The anchoring effect underscores how our perceptions can be shaped by seemingly innocuous data points that set the stage for our conclusions.

The anchoring effect is perhaps most vividly illustrated in the world of advertising and public messaging. Consider how a company might launch a new product, introducing it at a high price point before offering a discount. The initial price serves as an anchor, leading consumers to perceive the discounted price as a great deal, even if the product's actual value may not justify the initial figure. This strategy exploits the anchoring bias by manipulating consumers' perceptions of worth, deftly guiding their decision-making processes.

One notable case study exemplifying the anchoring effect occurred in the 2012 U.S. presidential election, particularly during discussions surrounding healthcare reform. Proponents of the Affordable Care Act (ACA) often cited the estimated cost savings associated with the legislation, presenting initial figures that framed the ACA as a financially sound solution. Opposition groups, however, countered by highlighting projected costs without providing corresponding context, thereby establishing a different anchor that influenced public perception. This conflict between competing anchors created a landscape of confusion, revealing how anchoring can be wielded as a tool in propaganda to sway public opinion by framing narratives in a way that benefits a particular agenda.

As we navigate the complex interplay of cognitive biases in the context of propaganda, it becomes increasingly clear that these mental shortcuts wield significant power over our perceptions and decisions. The way we process information is often governed by these biases, which can be exploited by those who seek to influence public opinion. Understanding these biases not only empowers us to critically evaluate the information we encounter but also equips us with the tools necessary to recognize when we are being manipulated.

In our increasingly interconnected world, where information is disseminated at lightning speed, awareness of cognitive biases—such as confirmation bias, the bandwagon effect, and the anchoring effect—becomes essential. It is a call to action: to remain vigilant, to question the narratives we encounter, and to strive for a more nuanced understanding of the information landscape. As we continue to explore the mechanics of propaganda and its effects on society, the insights gained from understanding cognitive biases will prove invaluable, guiding us toward a more informed and discerning approach to the information that shapes our lives.

By shedding light on these cognitive biases, we not only illuminate the mechanisms of propaganda but also empower individuals to reclaim their agency in an age of manipulation. The journey toward critical thinking and informed decision-making is one that requires ongoing awareness and reflection. It is a journey worth undertaking.

Chapter 12: The Mechanics of Persuasion: Understanding Propaganda Through Historical Lenses

In the age of information saturation, when messages bombard us from every conceivable direction, understanding the art and science of propaganda is not merely an academic exercise but a crucial skill for navigating modern life. Propaganda, in its most rudimentary form, is communication aimed at influencing the attitudes and behaviors of individuals and groups. Its historical significance is immense, having played pivotal roles in shaping societies and events that have left indelible marks on human history. This chapter looks into the historical context of propaganda techniques, exploring their utilization in significant events, and provides case studies that illustrate the ways cognitive biases can be effectively exploited to sway public opinion.

The narrative surrounding propaganda is ancient, dating back to the earliest civilizations whose leaders sought to control narratives to maintain power. However, its formal recognition as a tool of persuasion really gained momentum during the tumultuous years of the 20th century, especially during World War II. The war marked a watershed moment in the evolution of propaganda, where sophisticated strategies were employed by both the Axis and Allied powers to galvanize support, demonize enemies, and motivate troops. At this crucial juncture, propaganda was not just a supplementary tool; it became an essential component of warfare that shaped national identities and public sentiments.

As we explore World War II, we will witness how various propaganda campaigns were intricately designed to exploit cognitive biases—those inherent flaws in human reasoning that can shape perceptions and influence decisions. For instance, the use of emotional appeals, simplistic dichotomies, and authoritative endorsements were common techniques that fed into pre-existing biases, crafting a narrative that was not only compelling but also deceptively simplistic.

In addition to historical examination, this chapter will also spotlight contemporary political movements, where similar techniques of persuasion are employed on a global scale. The digital age has provided new platforms for propaganda, enabling rapid dissemination and amplification of persuasive messages. As political polarization becomes more pronounced, understanding how cognitive biases are leveraged in modern contexts becomes imperative. We will dissect specific instances where modern leaders and movements have invoked these psychological principles to sway public opinion, instilling a sense of urgency about the implications for democracy and societal cohesion.

Through the lens of these case studies, readers will garner insights into the psychological foundations of propaganda. This understanding serves not only as an intellectual exercise but as a mechanism for empowerment. Recognizing the pervasive influence of propaganda can arm individuals with the tools necessary for critical engagement, fostering a culture in which media consumption is approached with skepticism and discernment. It is imperative that we cultivate an awareness of our own biases, as they can cloud judgment and distort reality.

As we embark on this exploration, let us draw connections between history and the contemporary landscape, illuminating the lessons learned from past experiences and applying them to our current environment. By examining the role of propaganda, we can better understand the sway of narratives in shaping public opinion and the critical importance of informed skepticism in an era where information is both a privilege and a peril.

The role of propaganda during World War II cannot be overstated; it was a battleground of its own, where messages were crafted with the precision of military strategy. Both the Allies and Axis deployed a variety of techniques that tapped into the fears, hopes, and prejudices of their respective populations. The United States, for instance, established the Office of War Information (OWI), which was dedicated to disseminating information in a manner that would mobilize public support for the war effort. The OWI created films, posters, and radio broadcasts that aimed to instill a sense of patriotism and communal responsibility.

One notable campaign was the "We Can Do It!" poster featuring Rosie the Riveter, which encouraged women to join the workforce to support the war effort. This campaign effectively tapped into the cognitive bias known as social proof, wherein individuals look to others' behaviors to determine their own. The portrayal of women in strong, capable roles was not only empowering but also strategically designed to challenge traditional gender norms, thereby expanding the labor pool at a crucial time.

On the other side of the conflict, the Nazis employed their propaganda machine with chilling effectiveness. Joseph Goebbels, the Minister of Propaganda, understood the power of media in shaping public perception. His utilization of film, radio, and print media to promote anti-Semitic ideologies exemplified the manipulation of cognitive biases such as in-group favoritism and confirmation bias. The "Stürmer" newspaper, for example, fueled existing prejudices against Jewish people, presenting a narrative that painted them as threats to societal stability. By manipulating cultural fears and historical grievances, the regime was able to garner widespread support for its heinous policies.

This examination of World War II propaganda illustrates how historical context is vital in understanding the psychological mechanisms at play. The strategies employed during this period were not haphazard but rather the result of meticulous research into human behavior. Cognitive biases became tools of the propagandist's trade, allowing them to construct narratives that could elicit strong emotional responses while reinforcing existing beliefs.

Transitioning to contemporary political movements, one can observe a striking continuity in the use of propaganda techniques, albeit adapted to the digital age. The rise of social media has ushered in new avenues for the dissemination of persuasive messages, often blurring the lines between information, misinformation, and propaganda. Political campaigns, movements, and even nations now wield social media as a weapon, crafting messages that appeal to the biases of their target audiences.

Take, for instance, the 2016 U.S. presidential election, which was marked by the viral spread of information—both true and false—across social media platforms. The campaign strategies employed by candidates demonstrated a keen awareness of cognitive biases. For instance, one of the strategies involved the use of fear appeals to motivate voter mobilization. By highlighting threats—real or perceived— political operatives could stoke anxiety and urgency, leading individuals to support their cause out of fear of the alternative.

Moreover, confirmation bias played a significant role in shaping the information landscape. Social media algorithms curate content based on user engagement, often creating echo chambers where individuals are exposed primarily to views that align with their own. This phenomenon exacerbates polarization, as differing viewpoints are often dismissed or vilified, further entrenching biases. Digital propaganda campaigns have exploited this dynamic, disseminating tailored messages that resonate with specific demographic groups, leading to highly effective but divisive narratives.

The implications of these modern propaganda techniques extend beyond individual behavior; they raise critical questions about the health of democratic processes. When cognitive biases shape public opinion and drive political decision-making, the very foundation of a democratic society—an informed citizenry—becomes jeopardized. As individuals become pawns in a larger game of persuasion, the call for awareness and critical engagement becomes not just relevant but urgent.

In light of these observations, it becomes clear that empowerment through awareness is paramount. The psychological foundations of propaganda represent a dual-edged sword; understanding them can offer tools for both manipulation and resistance. As readers, we must encourage ourselves to recognize our own cognitive biases—those mental shortcuts that can cloud judgment and skew perception. By fostering an environment of critical thinking, we can develop strategies to challenge pervasive narratives and engage with media more responsibly.

To foster critical engagement, we must first learn to identify common propaganda techniques. This includes recognizing emotional appeals that seek to elicit strong feelings rather than rational thought, as well as spotting oversimplifications that create false dichotomies. When confronted with a persuasive message, ask questions—what is the source of this information? What biases might be influencing the narrative? Engaging with media through a skeptical lens enables individuals to make more informed decisions and resist the pull of manipulation.

Furthermore, cultivating an awareness of our own biases requires intentional reflection. Keeping a journal of our responses to news stories can help clarify how our backgrounds, beliefs, and experiences shape our interpretations. Recognizing moments when our emotions overshadow reason can serve as a powerful corrective, steering us toward a more balanced understanding of complex issues.

As we conclude this exploration of propaganda's historical context and its contemporary applications, it is imperative to emphasize the importance of informed skepticism. In an era characterized by rapid information flow and shifting narratives, individuals must become vigilant consumers of information. This means questioning the motives behind the messages we encounter, seeking out diverse sources, and remaining open to revising our beliefs in light of new evidence.

Informed skepticism does not equate to cynicism; rather, it signifies a commitment to truth and understanding.

By approaching information critically, we empower ourselves to navigate the complexities of modern life with clarity and purpose. The lessons learned from historical case studies serve not only as cautionary tales but as guiding principles for how we can engage positively within a democratic society.

As we stand at the crossroads of history and the present, let us carry forward the insights gleaned from these discussions. The legacy of propaganda is not merely a relic of the past; it is a living, breathing entity that continues to shape our world today. By arming ourselves with knowledge and a healthy dose of skepticism, we can reclaim our agency and contribute to a more informed, thoughtful discourse. In doing so, we honor the lessons of the past while paving the way for a future grounded in truth and understanding.

OUTRO

Empowering Public Discourse Through Knowledge and Skepticism

As we conclude our journey through the intricate world of propaganda, remember that knowledge is your most powerful tool. The techniques we've explored – from emotional manipulation to digital disinformation – are not relics of the past, but ever-present forces shaping our reality.

Your newfound understanding is not meant to breed cynicism, but to foster healthy skepticism. Question narratives, seek diverse perspectives, and always strive to uncover the truth beneath the surface. By doing so, you become not just a passive consumer of information, but an active participant in shaping public discourse.

The power to influence is now in your hands. Use it wisely, champion critical thinking, and become an advocate for informed citizenship in your community. Together, we can build a society that values truth over manipulation, fostering a democracy resilient to the perils of persuasion.